PC PROBLEM SOLVING MADE EASY

First published in the UK in 2010 by Which? Books

Which? Books are commissioned and published by Which? Ltd, 2 Marylebone Road, London NW1 4DF

Email: books@which.net

British Library Cataloguing in Publication Data

A catalogue record for this book is available from the British Library

ISBN 978 1 84490 109 8

3 5 7 9 10 8 6 4

The publishers would like to thank Sarah Kidner, Matt Bath and the Which? Computing team for their help in the preparation of this book.

Consultant Editor: Lynn Wright

Project Manager: Katy Denny

Designer: Blanche Williams, Harper-Williams

Proofreader: Corrine Ochiltree

Indexer: Ben Murphy

Essential Velvet is an elemental chlorine-free paper produced at Condat in Périgord, France, using timber from sustainably managed forests. The mill is ISO14001 and EMAS certified.

Printed and bound by: Charterhouse, Hatfield

Distributed by Littlehampton Book Services Ltd, Faraday Close, Durrington, Worthing, West Sussex BN13 3RB

For a full list of Which? Books, please call 01992 822800, access our website at www.which.co.uk, or write to Littlehampton Book Services. For other enquiries call 0800 252 100.

PC PROBLEM SOLVING
MADE EASY

▶ Contents

▶ PHOTOS, MUSIC & VIDEO

▶ KEEP YOUR PC HEALTHY

▶ ESSENTIAL SOFTWARE

▶ RESOURCES

EDITORIAL NOTE

The instructions in this guide refer to the Windows 7 operating system. Where other software or websites are mentioned, instructions refer to the latest versions (at the time of going to print). If you have a different version, the steps may vary slightly.

Screenshots are used for illustrative purposes only.

Windows 7 is an American product. All spellings on the screenshots and on the buttons and boxes in the text are therefore spelled in US English. The rest of the text remains in UK English.

All technical words in the book are either discussed in jargon busters within the text and/or can be found in the Jargon buster section on page 214.

INTRODUCTION

When your PC goes wrong, it can be a frustrating experience. Problems surfing the internet, lost photos, viruses, and devices that refuse to connect to your PC can leave you tearing your hair out and not sure where to turn for help. And that's where this book can step in to solve your computer blues. It's packed with advice that will help keep your PC running smoothly. From problems that occur as soon as you switch on your PC to error messages that stop you in your tracks, this guide will help you show your computer who's boss.

Using a PC needn't be stressful. With this book you can nip any issues in the bud with step-by-step instructions and advice that's easy to understand. Screenshots give you the visual back-up you need to understand exactly what to do, and jargon busters help demystify technical terms. And if you're really stuck you can contact the Which? Computing Helpdesk. Simply go to www.which.co.uk/computinghelpdesk and input code **PROBLEMS102010** where it asks for your membership number.

 For more information about Which? Computing magazine and membership, go to www.which.co.uk or call the Which? Helpline 01992 822800.

ABOUT THE CONSULTANT EDITOR LYNN WRIGHT
Lynn Wright is an editor and journalist with 20 years' experience in writing about computing, technology and digital photography.

HARDWARE PROBLEMS

By reading and following all the steps in this chapter, you will get to grips with:

▶ **Fixing a PC that won't start and recovering a crashed computer**

▶ **Understanding and fixing common start-up problems with your computer**

▶ **Tackling screen, sound and memory problems**

Hardware problems

MY COMPUTER WON'T START

If you're faced with a PC that simply refuses to start when you press the power button, the good news is that there's often a simple reason why it isn't starting. Some basic steps can quickly get you up and running.

Basic checks

If your PC will not start, a common problem is that it is not plugged in properly.

Check the power cables

With most desktop PCs you'll have at least two power leads to check – one for your monitor and one for the PC itself. Make sure that they're both connected properly. Also check the power leads for other equipment – for example, printers, scanners and external hard drives.

Check the power switches

Check that each device is turned on. Check whether your mains supply is working using the lamp test (see tip) and make sure that each component of your computer is switched on as well. Sometimes computers have two switches: one on the front and one on the rear (you'll usually find this near the socket for the power cable). Also check that the monitor power switch is on.

Check the power supply unit

If your PC is still not starting, it's possible that the power supply unit in your computer is no longer working and should be replaced. If you can, ask a computer repair shop to test it just to be sure. Replace your power supply if it has failed.

Looking for clues

If your PC does begin to start, but you are faced with missing screens and error messages or the PC freezes, then you may well have a hardware configuration problem. A further clue will be if your PC issues a series of beeps and refuses to work. A few quick checks can fix the problem:

1 Reconnect the monitor and check the video adapter.

2 Unplug the keyboard and mouse and try starting the PC.

3 If you have recently added an upgrade such as a memory module, then uninstall it (see page 22 for advice on memory) and try restarting.

4 Other system errors may come from non-compatible peripherals that need to be removed or loose connections. Check for bent pins, loose fits or stray wiring.

PC hardware repair

If no lights appear when you press the power button, there are no startup sounds coming from your machine, and the power supply is working, then this is a hardware failure in the PC itself. You'll need to have your PC repaired by an expert.

Jargon buster

Video adapter
A PC component that sends data from the computer to the screen and displays it as the image you see.

TRY THIS

To check that your PC is getting power from the socket, unplug it then plug a lamp in the same socket and turn it on. If it works, then you can rule out a power supply problem.

Jargon buster

External hard drive
A storage device that plugs into your PC. Useful for saving copies of important files or creating additional storage.

hardware problems

WINDOWS 7 WON'T START

If your computer has crashed, and when you switch it back on it refuses to launch Windows 7, it can seem a major problem. Many people simply reinstall Windows 7 – losing their data in the process – and if all else fails reinstalling Windows 7 is an option. See page 194 for advice on reinstalling Windows 7. However, there are things you can try before taking such a drastic step.

See page 194 for advice on reinstalling Windows 7.

TRY THIS

Aside from using the System Repair tool, you can also create and use a System Repair Disc that will enable you to put it into a CD or DVD drive, or plug into a USB port, and restore Windows. See page 178 for advice on how to do this.

See page 178 for advice on how to do this.

Using the Startup Repair tool

Windows 7 includes a Startup Repair tool that can fix many of the problems that stop your computer loading up and running Windows. The Startup Repair tool scans the computer to check for problems that prevent it from starting up, as well as identifying and fixing missing or damaged Windows system files.

How to start using the System Repair tool

If Windows refuses to load, you'll probably be faced with a black screen with white text, offering several options.

1 Remove all discs such as CDs or DVDs from your computer.

2 Power off, then turn on your computer.

3 Press and hold the **F8** key on the keyboard while the computer starts up. Ensure you press and hold **F8** before the Windows 7 logo appears.

4 Use the arrow keys on the keyboard to move the highlighted bar so that the option **Repair Your Computer** is highlighted.

5 Press **Enter** on the keyboard.

After Windows spends time loading files, a blue screen will appear with a message box titled System Recovery Options. In this message box, choose a keyboard input method, then click **Next**.

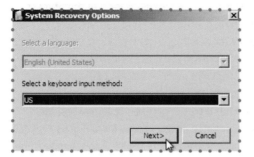

1 You need to log on as the administrator (see page 29) in the next screen, then the **System Recovery Options** menu will appear, giving you the following choices.

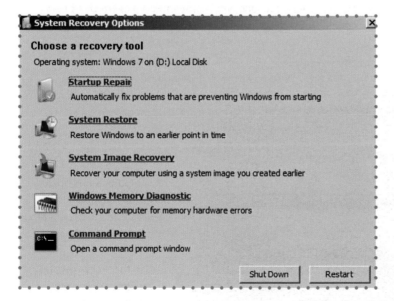

Hardware problems

System recovery option	Description
Startup Repair	This option fixes particular types of problems that prevent Windows 7 from starting. It can fix a limited range of problems such as missing or damaged system files.
System Restore	Choosing this option will turn back the clock on your computer and return Windows' system files and settings to an earlier point in time. For help and advice on System Restore, see page 13. Choosing this option will not delete or affect personal files such as photos, email or documents. However, you cannot undo a System Restore once chosen as an option, as it will return Windows to a previous state.
System Image Recovery	Only choose this option if you created a system image previously that you have access to. See page 194 for advice on creating a system image. This is a personalised backup of Windows along with all your files and includes all your settings.
Windows Memory Diagnostic Tool	This will examine your computer hardware for memory problems. For more help with memory problems, see page 22.
Command Prompt	Really only used by advanced users, this provides a text-based Command Prompt interface to run diagnosing and troubleshooting tools. For experts only.

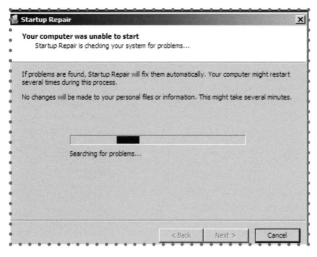

Running Startup Repair

Once you have an understanding of all the options, do the following:

1 In the **System Recovery Options** menu, click **Startup Repair**. This is probably the option at the top of the list.

2 Startup Repair will scan the computer, and this can take some time to complete. Wait until the scan has finished.

3 Follow the on-screen prompts, such as requests to Restore Windows to a previous state. If you see this message, click **Restore**.

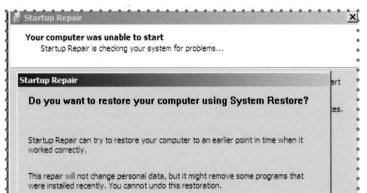

4 In the System Restore window, choose the most recent restore date, then click **Finish**.

5 If Startup Repair did not need to restore Windows, it will tell you if it successfully fixed the problem and will then restart your computer. Everything should load correctly and Windows should load and run.

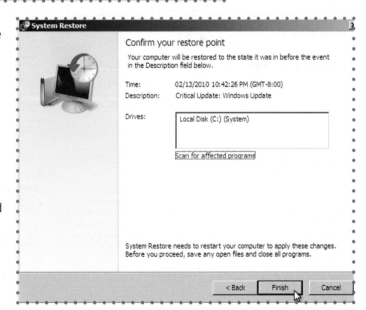

6 If Startup Repair could not repair the problem, it will tell you, along with advice and links to places where you might be able to find further help.

Hardware problems

WINDOWS 7 WON'T INSTALL PROPERLY

If you are upgrading to Windows 7 from a computer running a previous operating system such as Microsoft Windows Vista, or you are installing Windows 7 on a new computer, you can face a series of installation and activation problems. Here are a few of the more common ones, along with some solutions.

I'm not sure that my computer can run Windows 7
The first step is to check if your computer is capable of running Windows 7. To check the system specifications of your computer:

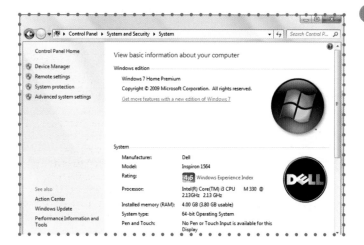

① Click the **Start** button, then click **Control Panel**. In the Control Panel, click **System and Security**. In the screen that appears click **System**. You can review basic information about your computer such as processor speed and memory installed. You can get further information about your graphics card, sound card and attached peripherals, too.

② In the left-hand pane, click **Device Manager**. To bring up further information about a piece of hardware, right-click on the hardware in the list, then select **Properties** to see more details.

I'm installing Windows 7, but it keeps getting stuck at 62%
If you are upgrading to Windows 7 from Windows Vista, you may find that the installation stops at 62% of the progress bar. The problem is a Windows service that can stop working during the installation.

1 Stop the installation, then in Windows Vista, click the **Start** button, then **Internet Explorer**.

2 Enter http://go.microsoft.com/?linkid=9693817 into the web browser address bar. This will download a fix for this problem.

3 Save and then run the program, then follow the wizard to fix the problem.

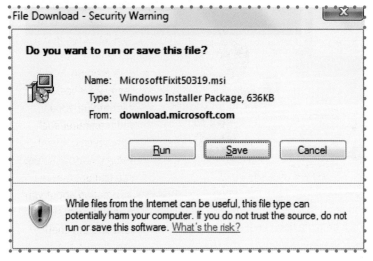

4 Restart the installation of Windows 7 again.

My computer endlessly reboots when installing Windows 7
If you are upgrading from Vista, this is a more common Windows 7 installation problem. After installation, you will see an error message that Windows 7 could not be installed and that Vista has been restored. The computer will reboot and attempt to start the upgrade process again, creating the same error message and an endless loop of rebooting. To fix this, follow the steps overleaf.

Jargon buster

Start Button
A round icon with the Windows logo in it, located in the lower left-hand corner of your screen.

Jargon buster

Processor
The main computer chip that controls and carries out the functions of a computer. The better the processor, the more a computer can do in a given amount of time.

Jargon buster

Wizard
A software helper that will guide you through a series of on-screen steps to help you set up or change the settings of a part of Windows, such as your firewall.

① Select **Vista** from the boot menu at startup, then insert your Vista installation disc in the CD or DVD drive.

② Exit setup when the Vista setup menu appears.

③ Click **Start**, then click **All Programs**, then click **Accessories**.

④ Right-click **Command Prompt**, then choose **Run as administrator** from the pop-up menu.

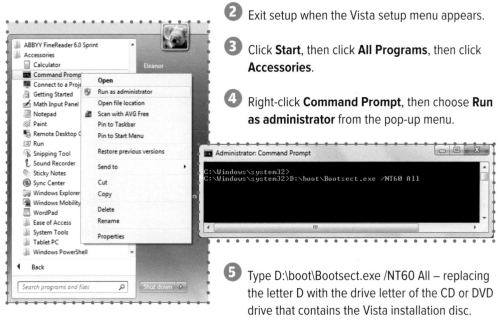

⑤ Type D:\boot\Bootsect.exe /NT60 All – replacing the letter D with the drive letter of the CD or DVD drive that contains the Vista installation disc.

⑥ Reboot the computer and begin the Windows 7 installation again.

I get the error message 'invalid product key'
You need to enter a product key when you install Windows 7 to confirm it is a genuine version. If you get this message it could be for one of the following reasons:

Possible problem You mistyped the product key.
Solution Try retyping the product key when prompted, taking extra care when entering the characters.

Possible problem The product key doesn't match the version of Windows 7 that has been installed on the computer.
Solution Check that the product key you are using is for the version of Windows 7 that has been installed on the computer.

Possible problem You are using a product key for an upgrade version of Windows 7, but there wasn't a previous version of Windows (such as Vista) on your computer when Windows 7 was installed.

Jargon buster

Drive letter
Each drive on your computer, such as the hard drive and CD drive, is assigned a different letter to help you recognize which drive is which. Typically, your internal hard drive is assigned the letter C, while DVD or CD drives will be assigned the letter E or F.

Solution To install an upgrade version of Windows 7, the computer must have Windows Vista or Windows XP already installed on the computer. If you formatted the hard drive during the installation of Windows 7, the product key won't work. You will need to reinstall the previous version of Windows, then reinstall Windows 7 again.

I still can't activate my copy of Windows 7

If you've followed the instructions to bypass the 'invalid product key' but can't activate Windows 7, then do the following:

1 Leave the box empty and click **Next**. This will install Windows 7 and it will run for 30 days before it needs activating.

2 Click the **Start button** in Windows 7, then right-click **Computer** and select **Properties**.

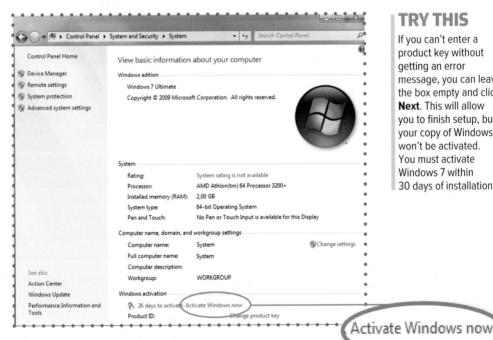

TRY THIS

If you can't enter a product key without getting an error message, you can leave the box empty and click **Next**. This will allow you to finish setup, but your copy of Windows 7 won't be activated. You must activate Windows 7 within 30 days of installation.

3 Choose **Activate Windows now**. This should present several options to activate Windows 7, including by phone. Call the number listed and follow the instructions. If you get stuck, a Microsoft support person will be able to help activate Windows 7 over the phone.

Jargon buster

Driver
Software that allows your computer to communicate with other devices, such as a printer.

Jargon buster

Icon
A small picture that represents an object or program.

SCREEN PROBLEMS

Your computer may be working fine, but some problems mean you can't get a picture on your screen, or it appears too big or small.

Check your drivers

Most screen problems are not caused by the screen itself, but by the computer's video card. The video card controls what is displayed on the screen, and the majority of screen problems are caused by missing or broken video card drivers.

1 Click the **Start** button, then click **Control Panel**.

2 In the Control Panel, click **Appearance and Personalization**, then choose **Personalization**, and click **Display**, then click **Change display settings**. In the screen that appears, click **Advanced settings**.

3 In the **Adapter** tab, click the **Properties** button.

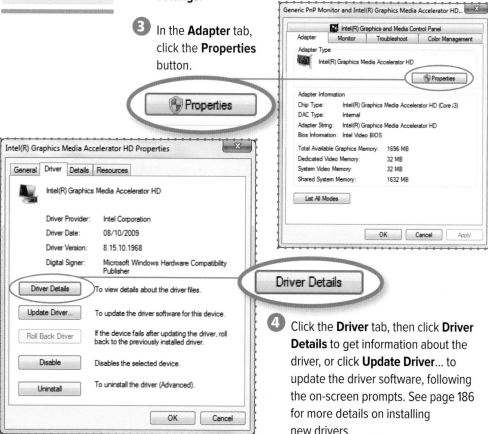

4 Click the **Driver** tab, then click **Driver Details** to get information about the driver, or click **Update Driver...** to update the driver software, following the on-screen prompts. See page 186 for more details on installing new drivers.

The picture on my screen looks too big or too small

The image shown on a screen is determined by the screen resolution. At high resolutions – such as 1600 × 1200 pixels – images look sharp, but icons appear very small. At lower resolutions, icons appear bigger but fewer items will fit onto the screen.

If your monitor is set to the incorrect resolution, the screen can appear too big, too small or blurry. It may not even appear at all.

TRY THIS

To get the best colour on your LCD monitor, make sure you set it to True Colour (32-bit colour) in the Monitors tab of the Adjust Screen Resolution setting found in the Appearance and Personalization Panel.

To change your screen resolution:

1 Click on the **Start** button, then click **Control Panel**. Under **Appearance and Personalization**, click **Adjust screen resolution**.

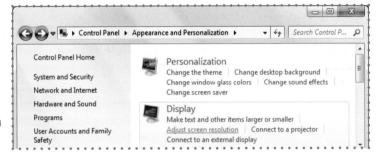

2 Click the **pop-up list next to Resolution**, choose the resolution for your screen (this is listed in the manual that came with your screen), then click **Apply**.

3 If you're happy with the new resolution, click **Keep**, alternatively, click **Revert** to go back to the previous resolution.

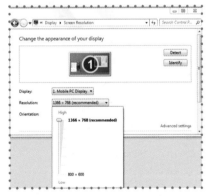

I've changed my resolution – but now I can't see anything

If you accidently choose a resolution that isn't supported by your monitor, the screen might not show a picture at all. To rescue your screen:

1 Restart your computer in Safe Mode (see page 26).

2 Follow the steps for changing your screen resolution in the 'The picture on my screen looks too big or small' above.

3 Restart your computer.

Hardware problems

Jargon buster

Taskbar
The bar running across the bottom of your screen, from where you can open programs and access the main Windows functions.

TRY THIS

If you don't see the Speakers button in your taskbar, then Windows doesn't detect any speakers connected to your computer.

SOUND PROBLEMS

If your PC and monitor are working fine, but the computer isn't playing audio correctly or there is no sound at all, there are several easy steps to try to resolve the problem.

The sound on my computer isn't working

First, make sure your PC's volume is turned up – click on the **speaker icon** in the taskbar at the bottom of the screen, or if you can't see the icon, click **Control Panel,** then **Hardware and Sound**, then click **Adjust system volume** and adjust the volume from there.

Once you've checked that the volume is turned up, check your speakers. If you're using surround sound speakers, the connections can be quite tricky, so refer to the setup instructions to make sure everything is in place.

Use the Windows 7 Playing Audio troubleshooter

You can try using the Playing Audio troubleshooter in Windows 7 to fix the problem, which checks for common problems with sound card, speakers, volume settings or headphones.

1 Click the **Start** button, then click **Control Panel**. In the Control Panel search box, **type 'troubleshooter'** and then click **Troubleshooting**.

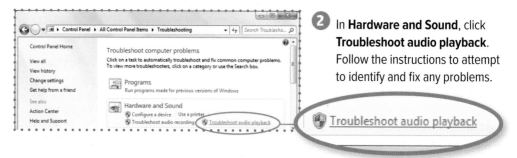

2 In **Hardware and Sound**, click **Troubleshoot audio playback**. Follow the instructions to attempt to identify and fix any problems.

If you're asked for an administrator password or confirmation, enter this now.

Fixing audio drivers

To check that your computer has a sound card or sound processor and that it is working properly, log in as an administrator (see page 29) and follow these steps.

1. Click the **Start** button, then click **Control Panel**. In the Control Panel window, click **System and Security** and, under System, click **Device Manager**. You may have to enter your administrator password.

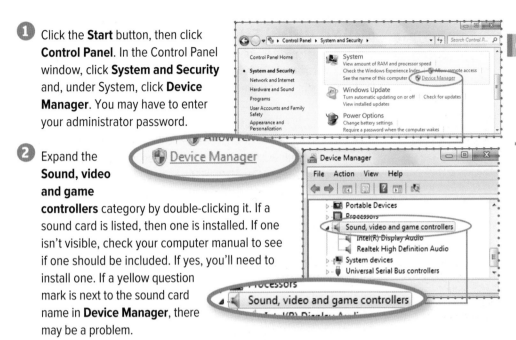

2. Expand the **Sound, video and game controllers** category by double-clicking it. If a sound card is listed, then one is installed. If one isn't visible, check your computer manual to see if one should be included. If yes, you'll need to install one. If a yellow question mark is next to the sound card name in **Device Manager**, there may be a problem.

3. With the mouse, right-click the name of the sound card and select **Properties** from the pop-up menu.

4. In the **Properties** box that appears, click the **General** tab, and then look in the **Device status** box to identify problems with the sound card. If there's a problem, you may need a new driver for the sound card. See page 186 for how to update and install drivers.

Other things to try

Other devices If your PC has a sound card, but it isn't listed as above, double-click the **Other devices** category and check if it appears there.

Laptop alert Laptops use integrated sound processors – these appear in the same category in **Device Manager.**

Physical volume control Some computers have physical, external volume controls such as a slider. Make sure this is not turned all the way down.

Music playback Lack of audio can be a software problem or a problem with your speakers. Check out the steps on page 160 (Music playback problems) to see if that solves your problem.

TRY THIS

The quickest way to change the volume for your computer speakers is to click the **Speakers** button in the notification area of the taskbar, and then move the sliders up or down to increase or decrease the volume of the speakers.

Hardware problems

MEMORY PROBLEMS

Some problems can be caused by your computer not having enough memory to perform all the actions it is trying to do, and this can make both Windows and programs stop working.

Signs of memory problems and low memory

If your computer is suffering from poor performance or display issues, or shows low-memory or out-of-memory notifications, your computer may have memory issues. An example symptom of low memory is when selecting a menu item within a program, when the menu disappears it leaves a blank area on the screen instead of showing the contents of the document you are using.

Memory problem programs

Some programs use lots of memory, which can leave your computer short of memory for carrying out other tasks. It takes just a few steps to find out which programs are hogging memory with the **Task Manager** tool. To see which program is using the most memory:

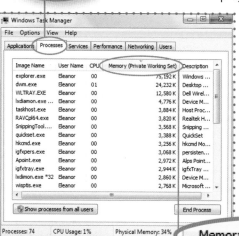

1 Right-click the **Taskbar** with the mouse, and choose **Start Task Manager** from the pop-up menu. Click the **Processes** tab. Sort programs by the amount of memory they are using by clicking **Memory (Private Working Set)**.

2 If one program is using lots of memory, either close it or check the software maker's website for an update or patch that may fix excessive memory use.

Increasing virtual memory

If you don't have enough RAM on your computer, Windows uses virtual memory – space on your computer's hard drive – as temporary memory. However, it's a lot slower than real RAM. Windows will automatically adjust the size of its virtual memory when it runs low on memory, but you can manually boost its maximum size.

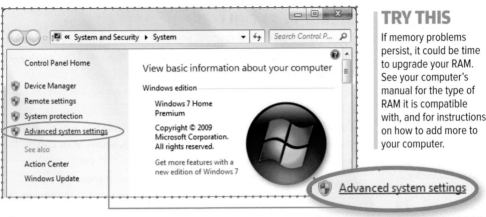

TRY THIS

If memory problems persist, it could be time to upgrade your RAM. See your computer's manual for the type of RAM it is compatible with, and for instructions on how to add more to your computer.

hardware problems

1 Click the **Start** button, then right-click **Computer**, and choose **Properties** from the pop-up menu. In the System panel that appears, click **Advanced system settings**. You may have to enter your administrator password at this point.

2 Click **Settings** in the **Performance** section under the **Advanced** tab. Again, click the **Advanced** tab, then under Virtual Memory click **Change...**.

3 Untick the box next to **Automatically manage paging file size for all drives**. With the mouse, click the drive (such as the main hard drive, or C drive) under the Drive [Volume Label] that contains the virtual memory – or paging file – that you want to change.

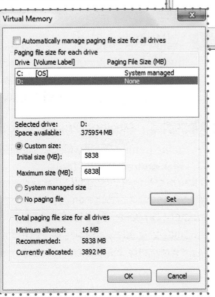

4 Click **Custom size**, and enter a new size in MB in either the **Initial size (MB)** or **Maximum size (MB)** box. Once done, click **Set**, then click **OK**.

TRY THIS

One way to tackle memory problems is not to open and run lots of programs at the same time. Closing a program once you have finished using it frees up memory that can be used to open other programs or increase the performance of Windows.

DISABLING STARTUP CONFLICTS

If your computer is experiencing startup problems, crashes or working slowly, it can be the fault of a startup conflict. This can occur because many programs are designed to start automatically when Windows starts. These often run invisibly in the background, so it is hard to know which of these startup programs are running – and not only can they use up lots of memory and slow Windows down, but can also lead to crashes during startup, known as startup conflicts.

What programs are running at startup?
A quick way to see which programs automatically run at startup is to look at the **Taskbar** at the bottom of your screen. Startup programs often add an icon to this area.

1 With the mouse, point at each program in the notification area. Click the **Show hidden icons** button to reveal any hidden icons, so you don't miss any.

Managing startup problems

If you suspect that a startup program is causing a problem, follow these steps:

1 Restart your computer in Safe Mode (see page 26) – this will start the computer without any startup programs running. If it starts well and the problem seems to be resolved, then there may be a problem with your startup programs.

2 Click the **Start** button with the mouse, then click **Control Panel**. In the Control Panel window, click **System and Security,** then click **Administrative Tools**.

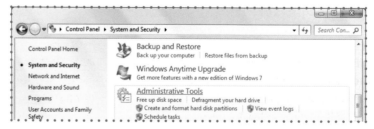

3 Double-click **System Configuration**. This controls various elements of the Windows configuration, including which startup programs load. You may be asked for the administrator password or confirmation by User Access Control (see page 54) at this stage. If so, enter it or confirm.

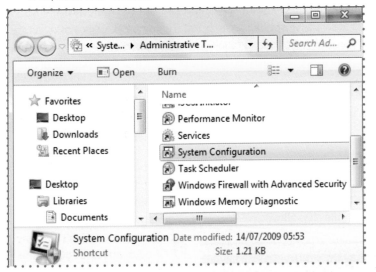

4 Click on the **Startup** tab. To stop a Startup Program from starting, select a startup program from the list and untick it. Continue working through the list, unticking programs that you don't want to automatically run when you start Windows. Click **Apply**, and then click **OK**.

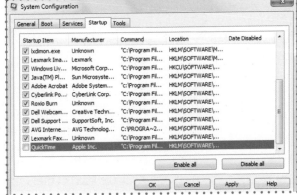

5 Restart Windows. If the problem is resolved, then the problem startup program was successfully identified and disabled.

If the problem continues, you will need to continue to disable different startup programs until you indentify the culprit. Once the problem program has been disabled, you can enable other startup programs that you may want by selecting a listed startup program and ticking it in the Startup tab.

Hardware problems

STARTING IN SAFE MODE

Safe mode starts Windows with a limited set of files and drivers, and it doesn't load startup programs. Safe mode is useful for troubleshooting problems with programs and drivers that might prevent Windows from starting correctly. If a problem doesn't reappear when you start in safe mode, you can eliminate the default settings and basic device drivers as possible causes. If a recently installed program, device or driver prevents Windows from running correctly, you can start your computer in safe mode and then remove the program that's causing the problem.

1 Remove all CDs, USB drives and DVDs from your computer, and then restart your computer. Click the **Start** button, then click the **arrow next to the Shut Down button**, and then click **Restart**.

2 Press and hold the **F8** key on your keyboard as your PC restarts – it needs to be pressed before the Windows logo appears on screen. If you miss it, let the PC restart then proceed again from the step above.

3 The **Advanced Boot Options** screen will appear. Use the arrow keys on the keyboard to choose **Safe Mode**, and then press **Enter**.

4 Log on to your computer with an administrator account (see page 29).

If everything started OK, you can then remove the problem program (such as one you recently installed) or disable recently added startup programs or remove recent drivers to stop the startup problems happening again.

When your computer is in safe mode, you'll see the words Safe Mode in the corner of your monitor. To exit safe mode, restart your computer and let Windows start normally.

WINDOWS 7 PROBLEMS

By reading and following all the steps in this chapter, you will get to grips with:

▶ **Solving Windows 7 problems such as logging on and common errors**

▶ **How to find and use features if upgrading to Windows 7**

▶ **Making your PC accessible, running older programs and removing programs**

ADMIN AND ACCOUNTS

When you log on to your computer, you log on with a user account. A user account tells Windows what changes you can make to the computer, what folders and files you can access, and what preferences, such as the screensaver, you use. If several people access one computer, it's usual for each person to have their own user account.

Each account has a name, a password and a type. As many Windows problems can be caused by user accounts or require that you log in with a user account such as administrator, it's worth understanding the different types of accounts.

Administrator account Used when you need to change something significant in Windows – many PC problems in this book require that you log on with the administrator account to fix the problem.

Standard account This is used for everyday computing and would be given to family members, for example.

Guest account Used by someone who needs to temporarily access your computer.

Choosing the right account

When you first set up your computer, you were required to create an administrator account. Once set up, it is best to set up a standard account for everyday computing, then log on to your computer with the administrator account to fix any problems. The Windows 7 log-in screen shows the different accounts available, as well as their type.

How do I switch account to the administrator account?

Using Fast User Switching, it is possible to quickly change from the account being used to another account, such as the administrator account, quickly:

1 Click the **Start** button, then click the **arrow next to the Shutdown button**, and click **Switch User**.

2 Choose the account from the list, and log in with your password.

Solutions to common user account problems

When I try to log on, I get an error message saying username or password is incorrect

There are several reasons why you may get this error message:

Mistyped your password Try retyping the password or if you have forgotten your password you will need to reset it. See the section on page 30 on resetting your password.

You have Caps Lock on Check your keyboard to see if the Caps Lock key has been pressed. User account passwords in Windows are case sensitive, which means that you will need to capitalize or lowercase each letter of the password as you did when you first created it. Make sure that Caps Lock is off and retype the password.

Logging on with the wrong account If you have several accounts on your computer, you could be inadvertently attempting to log on with the wrong account. Make sure you are logging on to the right account for the password you are using.

Your password may have been changed If you are using a standard account, someone may have used the administrator account to reset the password for your account. You will need to check with the administrator account holder to see if your password was reset.

▶ Windows 7 problems

Help! I've forgotten my password If you have forgotten your log-in password, there are several solutions you can try:

Use a password reset disc Insert your password reset disc into your computer (see next page for how to create a password repair disc), and follow these steps:

1 Click **OK** on the message that you have entered the wrong password when logging in, to close the message.

2 Click **Reset password**, then plug in the USB flash drive that is your password reset disc, or insert your password reset disc.

3 Follow the onscreen instructions to reset the password to a new password that you will remember easily.

4 Log on with your new password. If you lose this password, you can use the same password reset disc as previously – you don't need to make a new one.

Alternatively, if you have lost the password to a standard user account, log in to your computer using your administrator user account and reset the password for the standard user account.

1 Log in to the computer with the administrator account. Click the **Start** button, then click **Control Panel**. In the Control Panel, click **User Accounts and Family Safety**, then click **User Accounts**. You may be asked to enter your administrator password again at this point.

2 Click the **Manage another account** link, then click the user account name with the lost password. In the next screen, click **Change the password**.

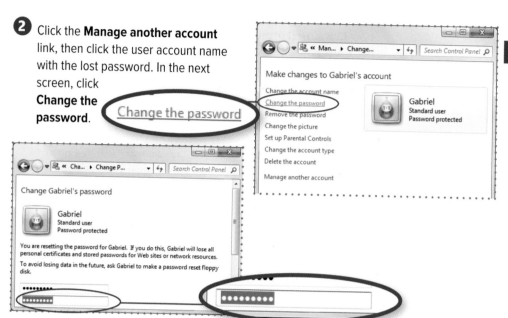

3 Type in the new password, confirm the new password, then click **OK**.

How do I create a password reset disc?

If you haven't already created a password reset disc, you should do so as soon as possible.

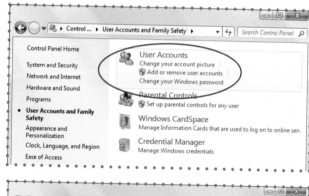

1 Insert a blank disc to be used as a password reset disc – this can be a USB flash drive, for example.

2 Click the **Start** button, then click **Control Panel**, then click **User Accounts and Family Safety**, then click **User Accounts**.

3 Click **Create a password reset disc** in the left-hand panel, and follow the onscreen instructions. Keep the disc in a safe place once created.

I have a fingerprint reader on my computer, but it isn't working

While a fingerprint reader offers a high level of security, if it stops working it can be difficult to log on to the computer. Try updating the driver – see page 186 for advice on updating and installing drivers.

I have too many user accounts – how can I delete one?

If you've created too many user accounts or need to remove one because it is no longer needed, follow these steps. It's worth noting that when you delete a user account you have the option of keeping all files created with that account, although email messages and other Windows settings associated with that account will be deleted.

BE CAREFUL

If you lose the password to your administrator account and you don't have a password reset disc or other administrator account, you will have to reinstall Windows again.

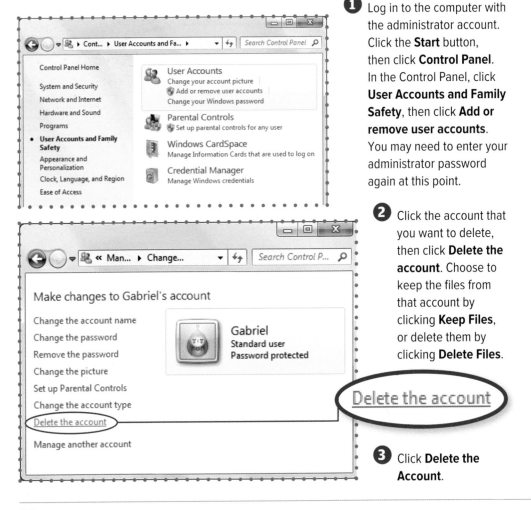

1 Log in to the computer with the administrator account. Click the **Start** button, then click **Control Panel**. In the Control Panel, click **User Accounts and Family Safety**, then click **Add or remove user accounts**. You may need to enter your administrator password again at this point.

2 Click the account that you want to delete, then click **Delete the account**. Choose to keep the files from that account by clicking **Keep Files**, or delete them by clicking **Delete Files**.

3 Click **Delete the Account**.

I'VE UPGRADED TO WINDOWS 7 - BUT I CAN'T FIND OR USE FEATURES THAT I USED TO USE

Upgrading to Windows 7 can be a daunting experience, especially as elements such as the Taskbar or Recycle Bin can seem to vanish or move, and some features don't work quite the same as previously. Here is a guide to finding and using common Windows elements that may have got lost when you moved to Windows 7.

Help! I can't find the Recycle Bin

The Recycle Bin usually lives on the desktop of your computer, but Windows 7 can hide it away. To show or hide the Recycle Bin on the desktop:

Windows 7 problems

Jargon buster

Desktop
The main screen you see when you start your computer. From here you can organize and access programs and files.

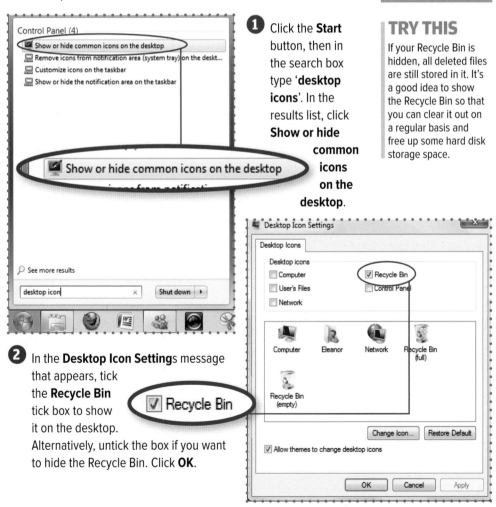

❶ Click the **Start** button, then in the search box type '**desktop icons**'. In the results list, click **Show or hide common icons on the desktop**.

TRY THIS

If your Recycle Bin is hidden, all deleted files are still stored in it. It's a good idea to show the Recycle Bin so that you can clear it out on a regular basis and free up some hard disk storage space.

❷ In the **Desktop Icon Setting**s message that appears, tick the **Recycle Bin** tick box to show it on the desktop. Alternatively, untick the box if you want to hide the Recycle Bin. Click **OK**.

Help! I can't find the taskbar

The taskbar normally lives at the bottom of the desktop, but it can get hidden away and there are several reasons why you might not be able to see it:

The taskbar was unlocked and has been resized This will make it hard to see even if you position the cursor over it.

Point to the area where the task bar should normally be at the bottom of the screen. The cursor should change shape to a double-ended arrow. Click and drag the taskbar border towards the middle of the desktop until it appears. Right-click the taskbar and choose **Lock the taskbar** to ensure it can't be hidden.

Auto-hide is turned on This means the taskbar will remain hidden until you position the cursor at the bottom of the screen on the taskbar border. If that doesn't work, try pointing the cursor at the left, right and top edges of the desktop, and it will reappear. To turn off auto-hide:

1 Right-click the **taskbar**. In the pop-up menu, choose **Properties**.

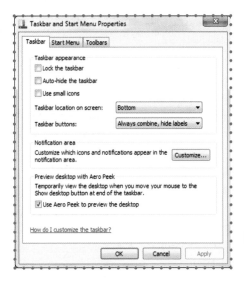

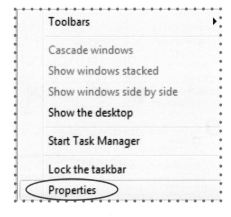

2 Untick the **Auto-hide the taskbar** tick box. Click **OK**.

You have more than one monitor The taskbar will only appear on one of the monitors – check the other monitor.

Help! I can't add or remove a desktop icon

Desktop icons are usually shortcuts to other programs, as well as actual folders and files. Depending on the icon, different things will happen when you delete it from the desktop.

The deleted icon is a shortcut The shortcut to the program will be removed, but the program itself will remain.

The deleted icon is a file or folder The file or folder will be moved to the Recycle Bin.

You can add or delete desktop icons for programs, files, pictures, locations and more.

How can I add a new desktop icon?

1 Find the program, folder, library or item that you want to create a shortcut for on your computer.

TRY THIS

To avoid accidently hiding the taskbar, right-click the taskbar and in the menu that appears click **Lock the taskbar.**

TRY THIS

Can't find the Start menu? Don't panic! You can always access the menu by pressing the Windows button, usually located in the lower-left of the keyboard.

Windows 7 problems

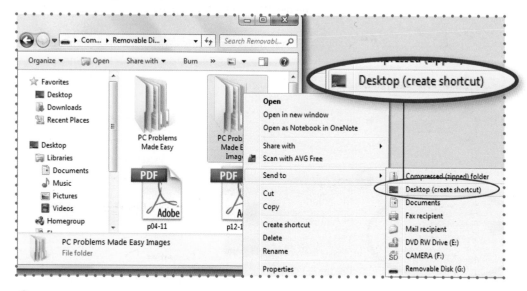

2 Right-click the item, then click **Send to**, then click **Desktop (create shortcut)**. The shortcut will appear on your desktop.

Windows 7 problems

Jargon buster

Wallpaper
A digital photo or image that is used as a backdrop to the Windows 7 desktop.

TRY THIS

To make any picture stored on your computer (or a picture you are currently viewing) your desktop background, right-click the picture, and then click **Set as Desktop Background**.

How can I delete an icon on the desktop?

1 Locate the icon on the desktop.

2 Right-click the icon, then click **Delete** in the pop-up menu. Click **Yes**.

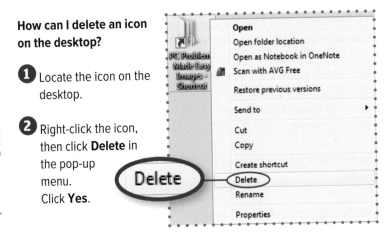

Help! I can't change my desktop picture

The image you see on your computer screen in the background is called the desktop background or desktop wallpaper. It can be a photo from the included images that come with Windows 7 or it can be your own personal photo. It can even display a slideshow of images – but not being able to change it when you've accidently set it to an image you don't want can be frustrating. To change the desktop wallpaper:

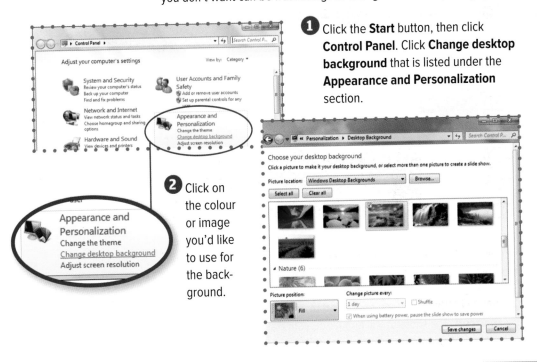

1 Click the **Start** button, then click **Control Panel**. Click **Change desktop background** that is listed under the **Appearance and Personalization** section.

2 Click on the colour or image you'd like to use for the background.

3 Can't find one you like? Click **Browse** to search for a picture – such as a family photo – elsewhere on your computer. Alternatively, click an item in the Picture location list to see other categories.

4 Double-click on the image you would like to become your desktop background.

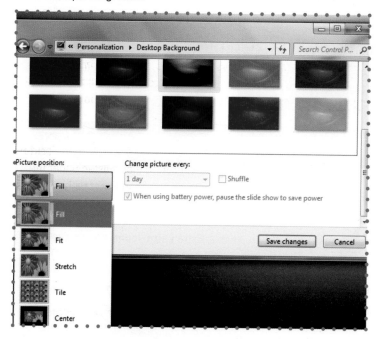

5 Click the arrow under **Picture position** and choose to either crop the picture to fill the screen, fit the picture to the screen, tile the picture, centre it or stretch the picture to fill the screen. Click **Save changes**.

Help! My icons of files and folders are too small or too big

Windows 7 shows files, folders and icons at a default size – but if you've just moved to Windows 7, you might think they are too small or too large. You can use the **Views** button in the toolbar of an open folder to change the size of icons.

1 Open the folder with files that you want to change the size of.

2 Click the arrow next to the **Views** button, then move the slider to change the size of the icons of your folders and files.

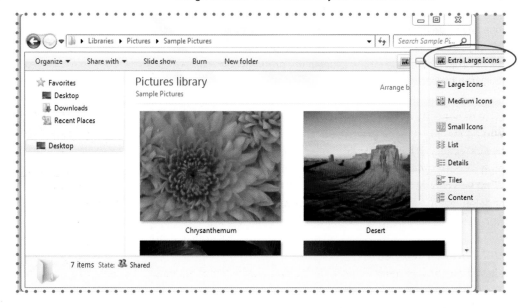

3 A series of settings, such as **Extra Large Icons**, can be clicked on the slider bar to jump to that setting.

You can move quickly between different types of views when looking at folders and files, by clicking repeatedly on the **Views** button instead of clicking the arrow next to it.

The five views are **List**, **Details**, **Tiles**, **Content** and **Large Icons**. Try them in turn to find the view you like the best.

COMMON ERROR MESSAGES

There are lots of potential problems that computers can face, and this book divides them neatly into the types of activity where you may encounter a particular type of problem. However, some problems are generic and there are common problems and error messages that you'll encounter no matter what you are doing. Here is a guide to some of the more common messages and what they mean.

{Program name} is not responding

What it means This means that a program you are running is taking a long time to complete a task. By clicking **Close the program**, you will lose any unsaved files that were being used by the program.
What you can do You can click **Close the program** to end it, but it can be worth waiting a little longer to see if the program does manage to finish the task.

Error moving file or folder

What it means If you try to move or delete a file that is being used by a program, such as moving a photo that is open in a photo-editing program, then you will get this message.
What you can do Close the program that is using the file, then move or delete the file. You may need to restart your computer if it doesn't work first time. See page 60 for more help with moving files.

Buffer overrun detected

What it means A program is trying to use more memory than Windows has allowed for it.
What you can do Click **OK** on the error message to stop the program running. Perform an anti-spyware and anti-virus scan as buffer underruns can be caused by malware, and ensure your security software is up to date.

Insert a disc

What it means Windows is expecting to find an optical disc – such as a DVD or CD – in the disc drive in order to carry out a task.
What you can do Check your disc is in the disc drive. If it is, then it may be that the driver for the DVD or CD drive needs updating. See page 186 for help with updating and installing drivers.

Windows 7 problems

Jargon buster

Buffer
A portion of computer memory used by a program as a temporary storage area for information being used immediately and then replaced by more information.

Jargon buster

Anti-spyware
Software that prevents and/or removes spyware.

Jargon buster

Anti-virus Software
Software that scans for viruses and removes them from your computer.

Jargon buster

Malware
Malicious software. A generic term for any program that is harmful to your computer, for example, a virus.

The system has recovered from a serious error

What it means You'll see this message if your computer has crashed and restarted. It was caused by a major conflict that required Windows to restart.

What you can do Not much, as it is usually a rare, non-repeating event. If it happens as soon as your computer starts up, then go to the section on Start up problems on page 10.

The Blue Screen of Death

What it means The Blue Screen of Death, as it is known, is a blue screen with white text that appears when your computer has a serious problem.

What you can do Your computer will need to be restarted and you should take note of the error code. Type this code into a web search engine to find information about what it means and also what fixes are available.

Windows 7 automatically restarts your computer when it experiences the Blue Screen of Death, not giving enough time to take a note of the error code.

To change this:

1 Click the **Start** button, then right-click **Computer** and choose **Properties** from the pop-up menu. Click the **Advanced System Settings** link.

2 Click the **Settings...** button under the Startup and Recovery section. Untick the **Automatically restart** box. Any new Blue Screen of Death will remain in place until you've noted the error message.

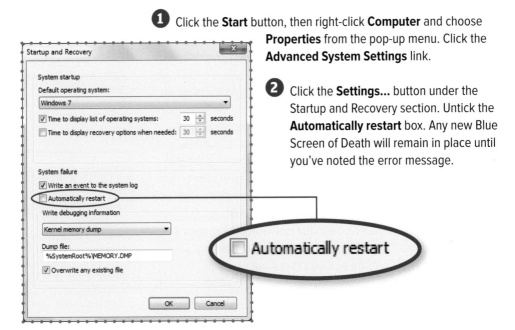

Problem with shortcut

What it means You've clicked an icon that was a shortcut to another program, but Windows 7 can't find the program that the shortcut links to. The program could have been moved, renamed or deleted.

What you can do Find the program that you want the shortcut linked to, then right-click it and click **Create Shortcut** from the **Send To** menu. This will create a new shortcut icon. Delete the original shortcut icon.

The following programs are still running:

What it means You've asked Windows to shut down, but some programs can't stop running because they have unsaved, open documents, or a program has crashed.

What you can do Close the program, saving any open documents.

The disk is write-protected

What it means Some disks, such as USB drives, have switches that prevent data from being written to the disk or content being deleted.

What you can do Ensure the physical switch is moved to a position that allows data to be written to or changed on the disk.

Device not ready

What it means You are trying to use a drive, such as DVD drive, before it is ready to be used.

What you can do Wait a while when you insert a disc so that Windows can ready it for use. If it continues to happen, consider updating the drivers for the device. See page 186 for advice on updating drivers.

The Compressed (zipped) Folder is invalid or corrupted

What it means You have attempted to open a compressed zip file, but Windows is unable to get at the compressed information inside.

What you can do If you downloaded the zip file from the web then download it again to see if it fixes the problem. If it is a zip file that has been sent to you, ask the sender to rezip the original information.

You are running out of disk space on C:

What it means You have nearly filled up the storage space on the C: drive with information.

What you can do The C: drive is used to store programs and temporary information, so when it is full it can cause problems. Consider archiving old files to another drive, such as an external hard drive, and removing unused programs.

COMMON WINDOWS 7 PROBLEMS

Windows 7 fixes many of the niggles and problems that previous versions of the operating system, such as Windows Vista, experienced. However, you may experience some problems and changes that are specific to Windows 7, especially if you are upgrading from a previous version of Windows.

Start with the new Troubleshooter

Windows 7 includes a new Troubleshooting feature that contains programs designed to automatically fix common computer problems,

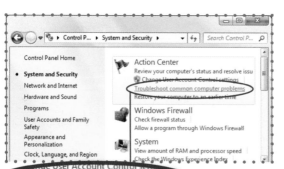

including using the internet, hardware issues and networking. You should use a troubleshooter as a first port of call as it may easily solve the problem for you.

1 Click the **Start** button, then click **Control Panel**. In the Control Panel, click **System and Security,** then click **Troubleshoot common computer problems**.

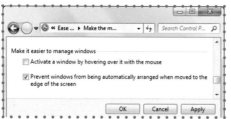

Look for how to use troubleshooters for specific problems throughout this book. Other Windows 7-specific problems that you may encounter are detailed over the next few pages.

Windows 7 keeps rearranging my open windows

This is an automatic new feature of Windows, called Areo Snap, and is designed to move and resize windows to help productivity. It can be annoying when windows move around without your permission. To turn this Windows 7 feature off:

1 Click the **Start** button, then click **Control Panel**. In the Control Panel, click **Ease of Access**, then click **Change how your mouse works**.

2 Under the **Make it easier to manage windows** section, tick **Prevent windows from being automatically arranged when moved to the edge of the screen**. Click **OK**.

Windows 7 has changed how my taskbar works

The new taskbar in Windows 7 uses a different approach to buttons, but it can be hard to tell if an icon is a pinned shortcut or a running program. You can restore it to make it more like previous Windows taskbars.

1 Right-click the **taskbar**, and select **Properties** from the pop-up menu.

2 Ensure that Taskbar Buttons are set to either **Never combine** or **Combine when taskbar is full**. Click **OK**.

3 To restore the previous Quick Launch toolbar, right-click the **taskbar**, then click **Toolbars**, then click **New Toolbar**. Type: **%userprofile%\AppData\ Roaming\Microsoft\Internet Explorer\Quick Launch** in the folder box, and click **Select Folder**. The Quick Launch toolbar should reappear.

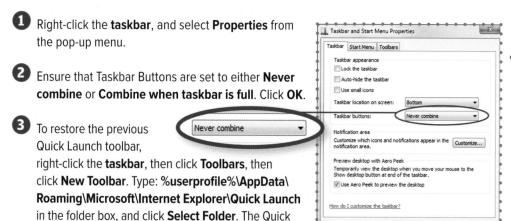

Windows 7 has hidden the Control Panel and Recycle Bin folders in Windows Explorer

If you're wondering where folders such as Control Panel and the Recycle Bin have vanished to when you click the Start button, then click Computer, Windows 7 has hidden them. To make them reappear:

1 Click the **Start** button, then click **Computer**. In the window that opens, click **Organize**, then click **Folder and search options**. Tick the **Show all folders** tick box, then click **OK**. The folders will reappear in the left-hand pane.

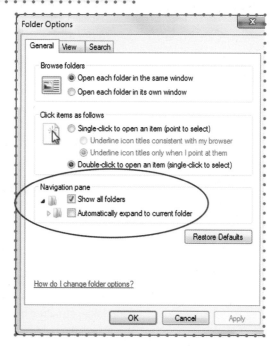

Windows 7 problems

Jargon buster

System tray
An area on your Windows desktop that displays program icons and alerts you when action is required.

Windows 7 has removed my photography, email and video programs

Windows 7 doesn't include some programs that were included in previous versions, with Movie Maker, Photo Gallery and Mail not included when you install Windows 7. Visit http://download.live.com to download the missing programs for free. For more details on these programs see pages 154 and 170.

Windows 7 has hidden the file extensions so I don't know what type a file is

File extensions, such as .doc, .exe, and .pdf, are hidden by Windows 7 to make everything look less cluttered. But they can be a handy clue as to the file type. To unhide them:

1 Click the **Start** button, then click **Computer**. In the window that opens, click **Organize**, then click **Folder and search options**, then **View**. Untick **Hide extensions for known file types**, then click **OK**.

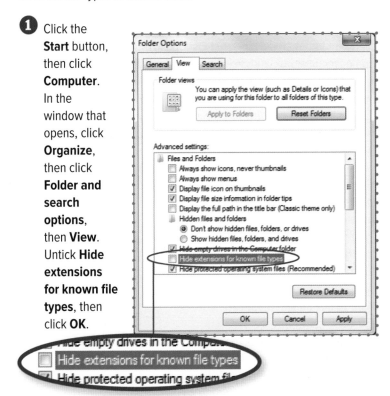

Windows 7 file navigation doesn't show me all my files

Windows 7 Explorer – used to find files on your computer – works differently from previous versions. Unlike previous editions, the left-hand folder structure doesn't expand as you navigate through folders and files in the right-hand pane. To return it to its previous behaviour:

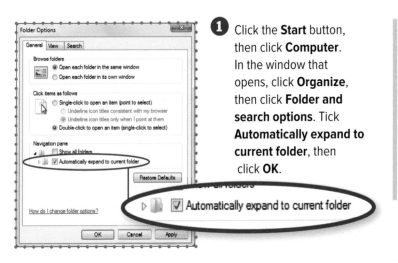

1 Click the **Start** button, then click **Computer**. In the window that opens, click **Organize**, then click **Folder and search options**. Tick **Automatically expand to current folder**, then click **OK**.

TRY THIS

Windows includes a handful of troubleshooters, but you can get more online by ticking **Get the most up-to-date troubleshooters from the Windows Online Troubleshooting service** tick box at the bottom of **Troubleshooting**.

Windows 7 problems *(vertical tab on right margin)*

Windows 7 keeps Windows Live Messenger on the taskbar

Even when you close Windows Live Messenger, Windows 7 will keep its icon on the taskbar rather than in the system tray, where it used to live in previous versions. This can take up valuable taskbar space, but you can reset it to behave as in previous versions:

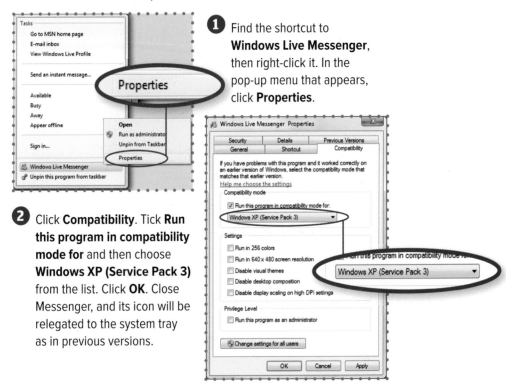

1 Find the shortcut to **Windows Live Messenger**, then right-click it. In the pop-up menu that appears, click **Properties**.

2 Click **Compatibility**. Tick **Run this program in compatibility mode for** and then choose **Windows XP (Service Pack 3)** from the list. Click **OK**. Close Messenger, and its icon will be relegated to the system tray as in previous versions.

MAKING A PC ACCESSIBLE

Computers are a great aid for those with accessibility issues, and with the right settings PC accessibility problems can be quickly solved.

I want to use the computer without a keyboard or mouse

If you want to use the computer without a keyboard or mouse, you can use either **Speech Recognition** that controls Windows using your voice, or, if you can use a mouse, display an on-screen keyboard.

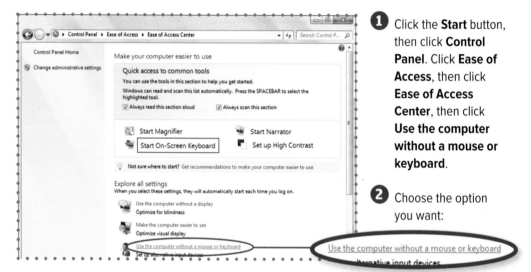

1 Click the **Start** button, then click **Control Panel**. Click **Ease of Access**, then click **Ease of Access Center**, then click **Use the computer without a mouse or keyboard**.

2 Choose the option you want:

Use On-Screen Keyboard This shows a virtual keyboard on the screen and you can use the mouse to point and click on characters as with a physical keyboard.

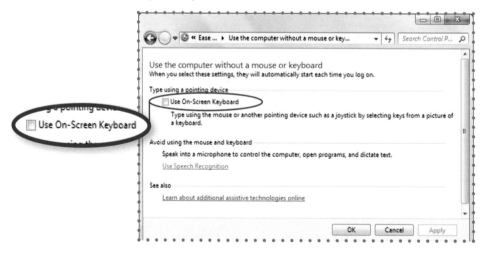

Use Speech Recognition You will need a microphone connected to your computer and this will allow you to speak commands to the computer, as well as dictate text.

I want my computer display to be easier to see

Computer screens can quickly become cluttered with distracting images, icons and information – but a few settings can make items easier to see, and can even have the computer describe what is happening to you by reading aloud.

1 Click the **Start** button, then click **Control Panel**. Click **Ease of Access**, then click **Ease of Access Center**, then click **Make the computer easier to see**.

2 Choose the option you want:

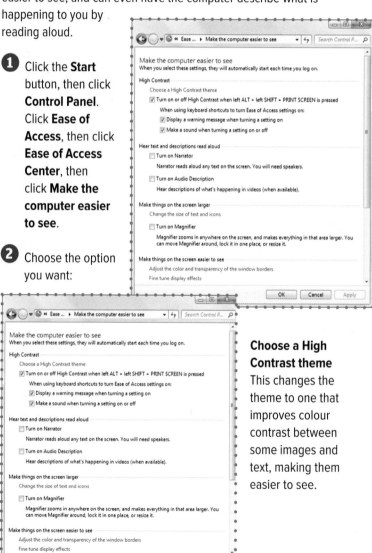

Choose a High Contrast theme This changes the theme to one that improves colour contrast between some images and text, making them easier to see.

Turn on or off High Contrast when **left Alt + left SHIFT + PRINT SCREEN** is pressed Toggle the High Contrast theme on or off with these keys.

Turn on Narrator This turns on the Narrator when you start your computer. It will read aloud on-screen text and items such as error messages when you use your computer.

Turn on Audio Description This describes aloud what is happening in videos that show on your computer.

Change the size of text and icons This changes the size of text and icons that appear on the screen, making them bigger and easier to see.

Turn on Magnifier This turns on the Magnifier that works like a traditional magnifying glass, enlarging the part of the screen that the mouse is pointing to.

Adjust the colour and transparency of the window borders This setting makes the borders of windows easier to detect.

Fine tune display effects Changes how some of the display effects are shown.

Make the focus rectangle thicker Makes the rectangle that surrounds the currently selected item in message boxes thicker, and so easier to detect.

Set the thickness of the blinking cursor Makes the blinking cursor in programs such as word processors thicker and easier to see.

Turn off all unnecessary animations Switches off distracting effects such as fading effects when you close windows.

Remove background images Hides all overlapping, irrelevant content and background images to declutter the screen and make the screen easier to see.

I want my keyboard to be easier to use

It's possible to use the keyboard to control the mouse, and use keys to give better accessibility to common Windows tasks and actions.

1 Click the **Start** button, then click **Control Panel**. Click **Ease of Access**, then click **Ease of Access Center**, then click **Make the keyboard easier to use**.

2 Choose the option you want:

Turn on Mouse Keys Allows you to use the arrow keys on your keyboard to move the pointer on screen, rather than the mouse.

Turn on Sticky Keys If you find pressing key combinations tricky (such as Ctrl+Alt+Delete at the same time to log in to Windows), Sticky Keys allows you to use a single key that you define instead.

Turn on Toggle Keys This shows a message on the screen each time you press keys such as Caps Lock, Scroll Lock or Number Lock, and prevents you pressing them without realizing it.

Turn on Filter Keys Tells your computer to ignore keys that have been held down for several seconds accidently, or keystrokes that happen in rapid sequence.

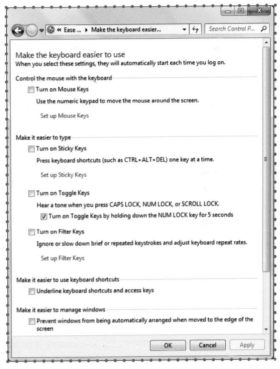

Underline keyboard shortcuts and access keys Underlines the key you need to press to control message boxes.

Prevent windows from being automatically arranged when moved to the edge of the screen Stops open windows from being resized and attached to the sides of the screen when they are moved there.

HOW TO REMOVE PROGRAMS

Many PC manufacturers pack new computers with programs you didn't order and might not want. These often include trial editions and limited-edition versions of programs that software companies hope you'll try, find useful, and then pay to upgrade to full versions or newer versions.

If you decide you don't want them, keeping the software on your computer might slow it down by using precious memory, disk space and processing power.

It's a good idea to uninstall all the programs that you don't plan to use. This should include both manufacturer-installed software and software you installed yourself but don't want any more – especially utility programs designed to help manage and tune your computer's hardware and software.

Utility programs such as virus scanners, disk cleaners and backup tools often run automatically at startup, quietly chugging along in the background where you can't see them. Many people have no idea they're even running.

Even if your PC is older, it might contain manufacturer-installed programs that you never noticed or have since forgotten about. It's never too late to remove these and get rid of the clutter and wasted system resources. Maybe you thought you might use the software someday, but never did. Uninstall it and see if your PC runs faster. For instructions, see page 51.

How not to remove a program

Just deleting the folder the program resides in won't work in Windows – it may cause future problems and it won't usually remove all the necessary files.

Similarly, removing the program's icon from your desktop or Start bar doesn't remove the actual program itself – you'll just be deleting the 'shortcut' that launches the program.

How to remove or change a program

The correct way to remove or change a program is to use the Uninstall feature in Windows.

1 Click the **Start** button, then click **Control Panel**. In the Control Panel, click **Uninstall a program**.

2 From the list of programs that appears, use the mouse to click the program you want to remove to select it, then click **Uninstall**.

3 Some programs will offer the ability to change or repair the program, as well as uninstall it. If you are experiencing a problem with the program, try clicking **Change or Repair** instead of **Uninstall**, and follow the on-screen instructions.

My program isn't listed

If you follow the steps above and the program that you want to remove isn't listed in the **Programs and Features** list, you should do the following:

1 Check the information that came with your program for advice on removing it.

2 Click the **Start** button, then click Computer. Navigate to the **C:\Program Files** folder as many programs install themselves. Many programs include an uninstall program in the program folder used to remove the program.

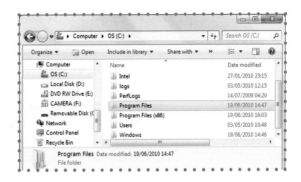

My program won't uninstall

If you still can't uninstall the program, try uninstalling it a second time as that can often succeed. Failing that, try starting Windows in Safe Mode (see page 26 for how to do this) and uninstall it then.

RUNNING OLDER PROGRAMS

Windows 7 is the latest version of Microsoft's operating system, and comes preinstalled on most new computers. Programs written for the previous operating system – Windows Vista – should work without problem, but programs written for an earlier version, such as Windows XP, might have difficulty working properly.

If you have an older program, you can try using the Windows Program Compatibility troubleshooter to see if you can make it work in Windows 7 – if you can't, you may have to buy the latest version of the program and check this has been rewritten to work with Windows 7.

1 Click the **Start** button, then click **Control Panel**. In the Control Panel search box, type '**troubleshooter**', and then click **Troubleshooting** in the results list.

2 Under **Programs**, click **Run programs made for previous versions of Windows**.

3 Follow the instructions in the troubleshooter.

Alternatively, it is possible to right-click a program's icon or shortcut and then click Troubleshoot capability from the pop-up menu.

Manually setting compatibility

Windows 7 offers the chance to fine-tune compatibility and adjust each setting individually. The table (right) shows the effect of each setting.

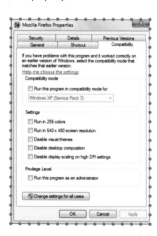

1 Find the program icon or shortcut, then right-click it. In the pop-up menu, click **Properties**, then click the **Compatibility** tab.

System recovery option	Description
Compatibility mode	Try this first if you know the version of Windows the program was written for. It automatically runs it with the right settings for that version of Windows.
Run in 256 colors	Some programs will only run with fewer colours on the screen.
Run in 640 × 480 screen resolution	Some programs will only run in lower resolutions that your monitor can support. This setting runs them in a smaller window with lower resolution.
Disable visual themes	A good solution if you experience problems with menus or buttons appearing strangely as it disables themes on the program.
Disable desktop composition	Switches off display features such as transparency effects. This can help fix display problems you experience with the program.
Disable display scaling on high DPI settings	If you are getting font problems when using large-scale font sizes, this turns off automatic font resizing.
Privilege level	Some programs will only run in administrator mode. You need to be logged in as an administrator for this option to be available. This setting runs the program as an administrator.
Change settings for all users	Applies any settings to all user accounts that use the computer.

BE CAREFUL

Do not use the **Program Compatibility troubleshooter** with older anti-virus suites or older disk utilities as this can result in a loss of data.

USER ACCESS CONTROL

I keep getting a pop-up message asking me if I want to continue? Is there something wrong with my computer?

If you use Windows, you'll get a frequent warning that will grey out the majority of your screen and presents a message that reads 'Windows needs your permission to continue' or similar.

This isn't an error message but a security feature to prevent accidental and malicious changes being made to important system files and settings. Any time you click on something marked with the icon of a red, green, blue and yellow shield, you'll get the User Account Control (UAC) message and you'll need to confirm this. If you're sure about what you're doing, click Continue, but if you're in any doubt, choose Cancel. Here's what the different shields mean:

 Multi-coloured shield symbol This symbol means that a Windows function or program that can affect other users of your computer needs your permission to continue. Check it's a program you want to run before clicking OK.

 Exclamation mark shield symbol A program that's not part of Windows needs your permission to continue. Check that you recognize the program and its publisher before you allow it to run.

 Question mark shield symbol An unidentified program wants access to your computer. This doesn't necessarily mean it isn't what it claims to be, only that it doesn't have a digital signature to identify it. Exercise caution and only run it if you got it from a trusted source.

 Red crossed shield symbol This symbol indicates that the program is blocked. To run this program you'll need to log in as the administrator and unblock it.

FILES AND DOCUMENTS

By reading and following all the steps in this chapter, you will get to grips with:

▶ **How to find lost and deleted files**

▶ **Fixing problems opening and saving documents and files**

▶ **Solving printing and font problems**

⊳ Files and documents

LOST FILES

You know you placed your important file or document somewhere – but faced with a mass of folders and windows, it can be hard to track down a missing file. Luckily, Windows 7 has some advanced searching capabilities that can help track down the file you need.

I can't find a specific file or a folder

Windows 7 has lots of ways to find files – and the best tactic is to mix and match methods to seek the misplaced file.

Using the Start menu search box

This is the quickest way to find a misplaced folder, file, email message or software program.

1 Click the **Start** button, then type the word or part of a word in the search box at the bottom of the Start menu.

2 The search results will start appearing as you type, with items appearing in the Start menu. The results are based on looking for a match for what you are typing with the text in the name of the file, text within the file, file properties such as date, and descriptive tags that you may have added.

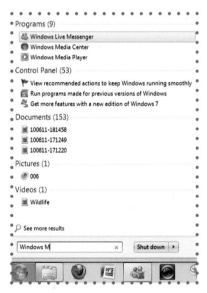

Searching within a folder or library

If you know roughly where the misplaced file is – such as in a particular folder or library, such as Pictures or Documents – you can refine your search to within these specific places. Using the search box within a folder or library searches through all subfolders within that folder or library, and looks for matches based on the file name, text with the file, file properties such as date, and descriptive tags.

1 Open and select the necessary folder or library, then type the word or part of a word in the search box.

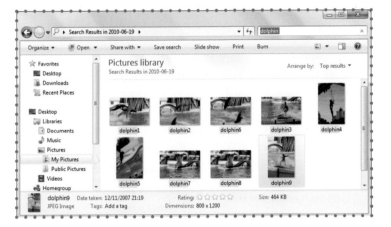

2 The search results will start appearing as you type in the current folder or library view.

Searching outside of a folder or library

If you need to expand your search beyond looking inside a particular folder or library, you can widen your search to include other locations.

1 Open and select the necessary folder or library, then type the word or part of a word in the search box.

2 Scroll to the end of the search results list, then under **Search again**, choose one of the following:

▶ Choose **Libraries** in order to widen your search to all libraries on your computer.
▶ Choose **Computer** to widen your search to every folder and location on your computer.
▶ Choose **Custom** to change the location to somewhere specific from the list of choices presented.
▶ Choose **Internet** to search on the web. This will open a web browser and take you on to the internet to search further afield.

Narrowing your search

While most people are familiar with using keywords to search for a file, such as 'bank letter', Windows 7 includes a series of search filters. These search filters can help narrow your search for a missing file, meaning you can search for particular dates, for example. To add a search filter when searching:

1 Open the hard drive, folder or library that you want to search, such as the **Pictures library** if you are looking for a specific photo.

2 In the search box, click a search filter such as **Date taken**:

3 Click an option, such as a date range, or a rough time such as **Earlier this year**, or a specific date.

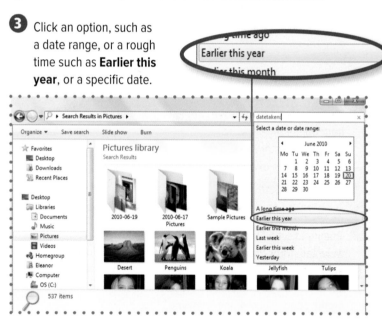

When you use a search filter, the search box will automatically add words to help narrow your search. It is possible to add extra search filters and different types, so it is possible to add other search filters by repeating the steps above to further narrow your search.

Different search filters will be available depending on what you are searching for and where you are searching, such as the Documents library or the Pictures library.

I'VE ACCIDENTLY DELETED AND LOST MY FILES

When you delete a file, it doesn't actually get fully deleted and lost – which is good news if you accidently delete a file and then change your mind.

When you delete a file, it is moved into the Recycle Bin. This is a storage space for files that you do want to delete eventually, but it gives you the chance to rescue them before you finally empty the Recycle Bin. To get back a file from the Recycle Bin:

1 Double-click on the **Recycle Bin** icon on the desktop. If you can't see the Recycle Bin, see page 33 for advice on making it visible on your desktop.

2 To rescue a particular file, click it once to select it, then click **Restore this item** on the toolbar. The file will be restored to its original location from where you deleted it.

3 To rescue all your files, ensure that no files are selected, then click **Restore all items**.

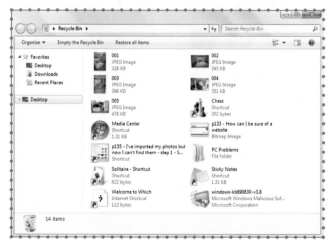

TRY THIS

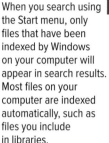

When you search using the Start menu, only files that have been indexed by Windows on your computer will appear in search results. Most files on your computer are indexed automatically, such as files you include in libraries.

files and documents

TIP

Widening your search to the entire computer will search all files, but the search will take longer.

I'M CONFUSED ABOUT MOVING FILES

Moving files and documents from one location on your hard drive – such as from the desktop to a library such as Documents – is easy, but it is easy to accidently put a file in the wrong place. Understanding how to successfully move files, and what happens when you move a file, can help solve some PC problems.

The most common way to move files is to 'drag-and-drop'. This means you use the mouse to point at the file, click and hold to select it, then – still holding the mouse button – drag the file from its original location to a new location, such as an open window of the Documents library. Once over the open window, releasing the mouse button will effectively 'drop' the file into its new location.

Depending on where you are dragging the file there are different results:

▶ Dragging a file from one folder to another, including a library folder, on the same hard drive will move the file from the first folder to the destination folder.

▶ Dragging a file from one folder to another folder, including a library folder, on a different hard drive, such as a USB drive, will copy the file to the destination folder. The original file will be kept in the same location as well.

▶ Press and hold the right mouse button while dragging a file to get a pop-up menu that allows you to choose to copy or move the file.

MORE ON MOVING FILES

Another way to move files is to 'copy-and-paste' the file, which means that the computer makes a copy of any file you select, then reproduces it in a location that you choose. The original file is left intact in its original location.

When copying-and-pasting a file, rename the new file that you create so you don't get the files confused. To use copy-and-paste:

TRY THIS

You can use the keyboard to copy-and-paste files. Press **Ctrl+C** to copy a selected file, and press **Ctrl+V** to paste the copied file into a new location.

1 Find and open the folder that contains the file you want to copy, and locate the file so it is visible in the window.

2 Right-click the file with the mouse, then choose **Copy** from the pop-up menu.

3 Find and open the folder that you want the copied file to be placed in, and ensure a clear, empty space is visible in the folder.

4 Right-click on the empty space within the folder and choose **Paste**. A copy of the original file will then appear in the folder.

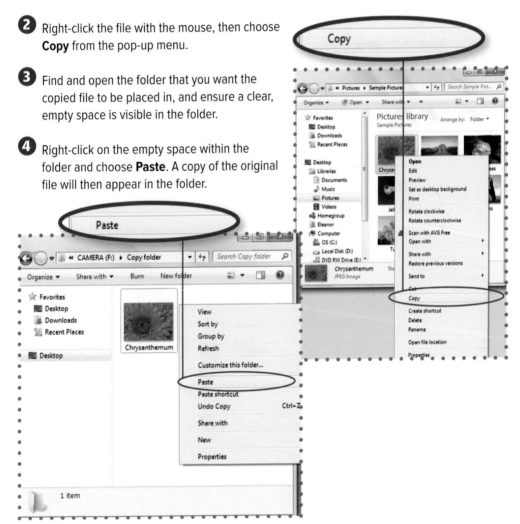

files and documents

I CAN'T SUCCESSFULLY OPEN FILES

Opening a file or document in Windows 7 is usually straightforward. Locate the file, then double-click it to open both the program you need to view the file and the file itself. But sometimes clicking a file opens the incorrect program or refuses to open at all.

When I open a file, it opens in the wrong program

All files are associated with – or linked to – a specific program. For example, a photo file (such as a file ending in .jpg or .tif) will usually open **Picture Viewer** when double-clicked. But if you want to open photos in a different program – such as Adobe Photoshop Elements for editing it – you need to specify which program to open the file in.

1 Locate the file in Windows that you wish to open.

2 Right-click the file. In the pop-up menu, click **Open with**, then click the name of the program you want to open the file in. That program will then launch rather than the default program, along with the file.

When I double-click a file, I get a 'Windows can't open this file' error message

If a file isn't associated with – or linked to – a specific program, Windows won't be able to open the file. You may be trying to open a file that is not capable of being opened by any program installed on your computer.

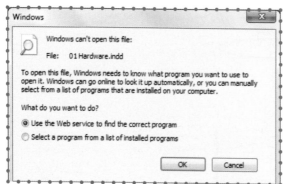

1 Double-click the file you want to open.

2 In the error message box that appears, click **Use the Web service to find the correct program**, then click **OK**.

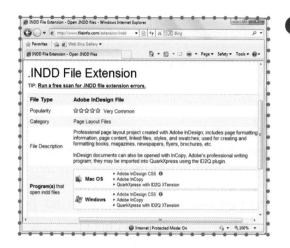

3 You will get a list of suggested programs to install in order to view the file, and you can expand your search further onto the web.

How can I always ensure that a certain file is opened in a specific program?

If you want to ensure that a certain file, such as a text document, always opens in Microsoft Word, when double-clicked:

1 Locate the file in Windows.

2 Right-click the file, then in the pop-up menu point to **Open with** and then click **Choose default program...**.

3 Click the program from the list that you want the file to open in from now on.

4 Tick the **Always use the selected program to open this kind of file** tick box, then click **OK**.

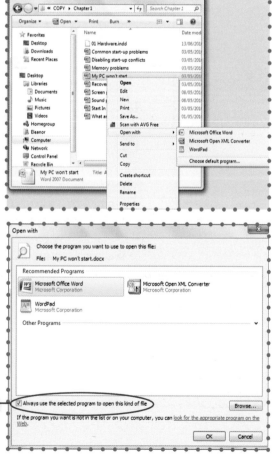

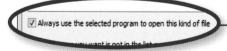

Files and documents

SAVING FILES

Saving files is one of the most important activities you can perform. If you save a file that you are working on often, if the program crashes or the computer experiences a power cut, you will not have wasted valuable time and you'll have an up-to-date copy of your file.

How can I save a file properly?
Saving a file always takes place in the program you are using to work on the file, rather than in Windows.

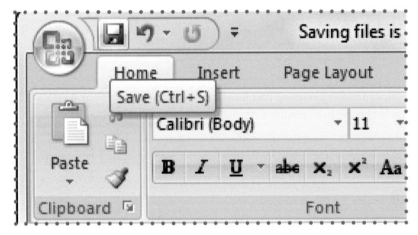

1 In the program with the file open, click the **File** menu, then click **Save**, or click the icon of a disk in some programs.

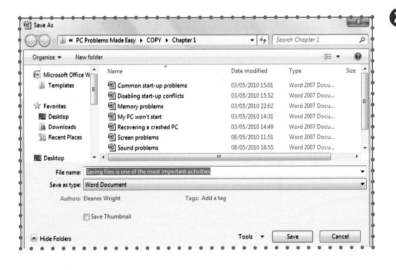

2 If this is the first time you are saving the file, navigate to the location you want to save it to and type in a name for the file. Then click **Save**. If the file has been saved before, then it will update the previously saved file.

How can I save a new version and protect my previous file?

Sometimes you might want to open a file, work on it, then save the new, updated version as a different file, rather than updating and overwriting the older file. This means you retain the original file if you need to go back and work on it again in a different way, as well as creating a new, updated version of the file you have worked on.

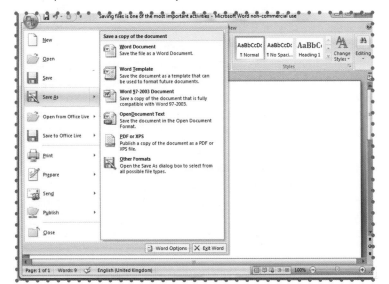

1 In the program with the file open, click the **File** menu, then click **Save As**.

2 Navigate to the location you want to save the file, then enter a new name for the file. Then click **Save**.

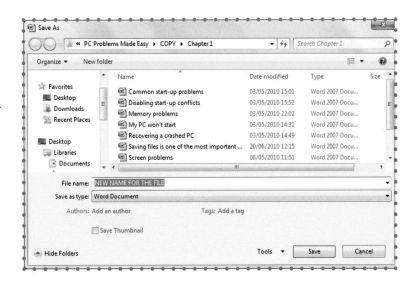

My file won't save at all

If you are following the previous steps and you can't save the file, it could be due to one of the following issues:

The software is a trial version Some software trials allow you to use the software to open and create files, but you can't save your work. This is often shown by a greyed-out **Save** option on the **File** menu. You need to upgrade to the full version.

The hard drive is protected If you are trying to save to a USB drive, check it is not physically write-protected – there is usually a mechanical slider on the side of the USB driver that can toggle between a locked or unlocked padlock symbol. You cannot save files to media such as pre-recorded CDs or DVDs.

The program isn't ready to save Check that there are no open message windows awaiting your input, such as confirmation of an action. The program may be awaiting a response from you before it can continue with saving.

FONT PROBLEMS

Fonts or typefaces are the digital letter and character styles of all text on your computer. Popular fonts include Times, Helvetica and Arial.

I can't see a new font that I just installed in my font menu

Ensure that you close and then reopen any programs that were open when you installed a new font, so that they can register the new font.

Check if the font is compatible with your software – refer to the software program's manual for guidance on the font types it supports.

Some fonts require both a bitmap screen font file and an outline printer file. If the bitmap font file is missing, it can cause the font not to appear in a font menu or the text on screen to look jagged. Reinstall the font or contact the font manufacturer to obtain the bitmap version.

My printed text looks different to my onscreen text

Some fonts used on the screen are not supported by certain printers. A possible solution is to change the font to a TrueType font – these font types will always look the same on screen and in print.

Ensure that you didn't resize the font on screen – try resizing it again to a different size and see if the printed version better matches the onscreen type.

Try printing with the same font from another file or document – if the problem repeats, then the problem is probably with the font. Reinstall the font.

My fonts look funny when I open a document from another computer

Unless you have access to the same fonts that were used to originally create the document, you won't be able to see the font correctly, and Windows will instead show it in a different font that you do have, or even not show any text at all.

To fix this, you can embed some TrueType fonts into the document so that the font effectively travels with the document, ensuring that text can be viewed without problems on any computer. Check the **Help** section of your document-creation software for advice on how to embed fonts.

Jargon buster

Bitmap screen font file
Shows a digital version of a letter made up of tiny dots called pixels. While this is suitable for the screen, when printed out a bitmap file tends to look jagged.

TIP

Get a TrueType version of most fonts from a typeface company such as www.fonts.com.

PRINTER PROBLEMS

My text isn't fitting on the printed page properly

Check paper size and font size If you make the font size too big, or set the incorrect paper size in the **Print options** box when you print your page, text can run off the edges.

Set margins correctly In the **Print options** box, ensure that the margins of the page are set correctly. Many printers can't print to the edge of a piece of paper, and so require some margin free of text around the outside.

Check document size If the document you are creating is larger than the paper size in the printer, it might not print properly. For example, if you choose an A3 document but print on A4 paper, the printer might not shrink it properly to fit on the smaller, A4 paper size.

My printer is refusing to print anything

The first port of call is to run the Printer troubleshooter in Windows 7.

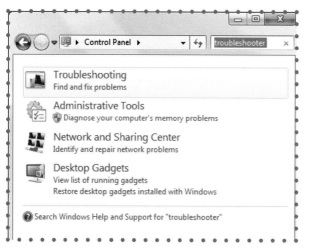

1 Click the **Start** button, then click **Control Panel**. In the Control Panel search box type '**troubleshooter**', then click **Troubleshooting**.

2 Under **Hardware and Sound**, click **Use a printer**.

3 Follow the steps that appear on screen, and follow any recommended fixes.

If that doesn't fix the printing problem, then you may have a problem with the driver of your printer. See page 186 for advice on updating and installing drivers.

I've got a 'Print spooler' error message

The print spooler is another name for the area of the hard drive on your computer that Windows uses to temporarily store the documents being sent to the printer. It keeps them in this space until the printer is ready to accept and print the document.

The simplest way to restart the spooler is to save your work and restart the computer. You can also try these steps:

1 Click the **Start** button, then click **Control Panel**. In the Control Panel search box, type '**administrative tools**'. Click **Administrative Tools** from the results list.

2 Double-click **Services**. You may have to enter your administrator password at this point.

3 Right-click the **Print Spooler** service, then click **Properties**. On the **General** tab, ensure that **Automatic** is selected beside **Startup type**.

4 If the print spooler service is not running, click **Start under Service status**, then click **OK**. You may have to enter your administrator password at this point.

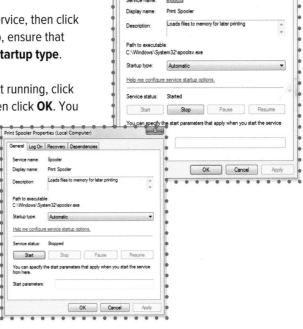

The print spooler will now begin working again.

I want to add a network printer but it's not showing up

If your computer can't find the printer on your home network that you want to use, you will need to help Windows detect and add the printer manually.

① Click the **Start** button, then click **Devices and Printers** on the Start menu. Click **Add a printer** in the window that appears.

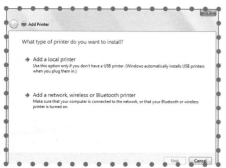

② In the Add printer wizard, choose **Add a network, wireless or Bluetooth printer**.

③ When you see the Searching for available printers page, click **The printer that I want isn't listed**.

④ On the **Find a printer by name or TCP/IP address path**, choose how you want to find the printer based on the location or type of printer, then click **Next**.

⑤ Follow the remaining steps in the printer wizard, then click **Finish** when done.

Jargon buster

Bluetooth
A type of short range, wireless connection for transferring data between devices.

NETWORK PROBLEMS

By reading and following all the steps in this chapter, you will get to grips with:

▶ **Tackling network security problems and network log-on problems**

▶ **Solving problems connecting to the internet and Wi-Fi networks**

▶ **Troubleshooting slow internet and network problems**

Network problems

HOW CAN I SECURE MY NETWORK?

Wireless networks in the home are far more convenient than traditional, wired ones, but they bring with them certain security risks. It's important that you take precautions to stop people connecting to your network or even changing your network settings, without your knowledge.

If you don't implement proper security measures, anyone within range (such as neighbours and passers-by) who has a wireless-enabled device could piggyback your broadband internet connection – or possibly gain access to your PCs. So don't forget to enable encryption when you install your network.

I'm unsure about what encryption I should be using
There are two main kinds of encryption: WEP (Wired Equivalent Privacy) or WPA (Wi-Fi Protected Access). Both use a system that prevents any wireless device without the correct authentication key from accessing the network.

WPA is newer and slightly stronger, as it scrambles the encryption key, but check first that all the devices on your network can use it before choosing this option.

The first step is to turn on encryption on your wireless router by going to the configuration utility, locating the security settings and following the instructions there (see How can I secure my network?, page 73).

Once you've done this, make a note of the authorization key and type this in when asked to during the setup for each of your other wireless devices.

All wireless networks have a name (sometimes called the SSID) that you can change when you set up your router. Change it to something that doesn't give any clues to your identity or to the type of router that you're using.

For example, don't call it by the name of your router. You can also tell the router not to broadcast the network name (or SSID). This makes it more difficult for anyone looking for a network to connect to it. If you won't often be connecting new devices to your network, consider turning off the router's broadcast SSID option.

How can I secure my network?

Most wireless home networks are made up of a router, which you can access using a wireless-enabled computer, and a web browser. You can use this to access your router and change settings, including security settings. Each router is different, so refer to the manual that came with the router for security settings. Some general settings are detailed below.

Click on the **Start** button, then choose **All Programs** and launch **Internet Explorer** or another web browser. Enter the address of your router into the browser's address bar. This is a number listed in your router instruction manual. For many brands, the number you need to enter is 192.168.1.1. Press **Enter**.

You'll see a page that looks like a webpage, which is hosted in the router. From here you can make changes to the router.

To change the default password, click the **Administration** tab (this may vary between routers). Many routers come with 'weak' passwords like 'admin', making it easy to guess. If someone gains access to your network, they may be able to guess the router's password if it hasn't been changed and they can then change any of your network settings.

Finally, you need to encrypt your network. Your router instruction manual should show you how. Bear in mind that the older system, known as WEP, isn't as secure as the newer system (called WPA).

Network problems

TRY THIS

You can reset the router to its original settings if you make a mistake or forget the setup password. You can do this by holding down the reset button for a count of 10 seconds on most routers.

How can I safely share my files with other computers?

Once your network is set up, you'll need to set all your computers to share their files and folders. Here's how to do this in Windows 7:

1 Click the **Start** button, then **Computer**. Right-click on the folder containing the files you want to share, and select **Share with**. A further pop-up menu will give you a list of your network choices, such as Homegroup. Choose the group to share with, choosing to either (Read), which only lets others see inside the folder, or (Read/Write), which also allows others to add files to the folder.

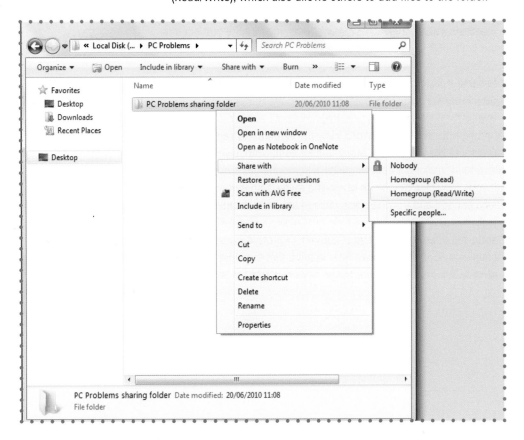

2 It's possible to allow access to a whole drive but we don't recommend it for security reasons. To do so, browse **My Computer**, right-click on the drive and follow the same process as before.

How do I know if a wireless network is secure?

There is no way to guarantee complete security on a wireless network. However, there are precautions you can take to help minimize security risks when you use a wireless network.

▶ Whenever possible, only connect to wireless networks that require a network security key or have some other form of security, such as a certificate. The information sent over these networks is encrypted, which can help protect your computer from unauthorized access. When you view available wireless networks in Connect to a Network, wireless networks that do not have security enabled will be identified with a yellow shield icon.

▶ Before you connect to a network provided by a wireless internet service provider (ISP), such as a public network in a coffee shop or airport, read the privacy statement carefully and make sure that you understand which files, if any, are saved to your computer and what type of information the network provider collects from your computer.

▶ If you connect to a network that's not secure, be aware that someone with the right tools can see everything that you do, including the websites you visit, the documents you work on, and the usernames and passwords you use. Make sure that you don't work on any company-sensitive information or visit password-protected areas of your business network while you're connected to that network.

TRY THIS

Your router will be able to tell you all sorts of information about what it's doing. Clicking on the **Status** tab on the router's home page will let you see, for instance, whether your ADSL connection is active, and at what speed, or which computers are connected.

TIP

Name your network so it won't reveal your identity, location or the make of your router.

▶ Network problems

I CAN'T CONNECT TO MY NETWORK

With home networks increasingly an everyday feature of home computing, they make it easy to swap files between computers and print documents to networked printers.

I can't connect to my home network

Run the Network troubleshooter to help find and fix any of the more likely problems with Windows 7 on your computer. See page 84 for using the Network troubleshooter.

1 If you've just installed new software, this can cause some of your connection settings to change. To see if they have changed:

2 Click the **Start** button and click **Control Panel**. In the Control Panel search box, type '**adapter**'. Click **View connections** under the **Network and Sharing Center**. Right-click the connection, then click **Properties** from the pop-up menu. Check to see if your network settings have changed.

3 If you are using a home network with a homegroup, ensure that the computer you are trying to connect to has been added to the homegroup as a recognized computer. To do this:

4 Click the **Start** button and click **Control Panel**. In the Control Panel search box, type '**homegroup**'. Click **Choose homegroup and sharing options**, and click the **Create a homegroup** button. See page 79 for help on creating a homegroup.

5 Make sure that you have enabled file and printer sharing on your home network. To do this:

6 Click the **Start** button and click **Control Panel**. In the Control Panel search box, type '**homegroup**'. Tick the items you want to share in the **Share libraries and printers** section.

7 Check your router, especially if it is slightly older. New networking features in Windows 7 can make older routers not work with newer computers. To find out if your router is compatible, download the Internet Connectivity Evaluation Tool from www.microsoft.com/windows/using/tools/igd on another computer, then install it on the computer that can't connect to the internet.

8 Check that all your cables, such as your Ethernet cable, are securely plugged into both your computer and the router. If in doubt, unplug then plug each cable back in.

> **Jargon buster**
>
> **Ethernet**
> A means of connecting computers together using cables – a common method for networking computers.

I can't connect to other computers on the network
If you can't connect to other computers on the network or share files and printers with them, it could be that Network discovery is switched off in Windows 7.

1 Click the **Start** button, then click **Control Panel**. Type '**network**' into the Control Panel search box, then click **Network and Sharing Center**. In the left panel, click **Change advanced sharing settings**.

2 Expand the network profile by clicking the arrow, then click **Turn on network discovery**, then click **Save changes**. You may have to enter your administrator password at this point.

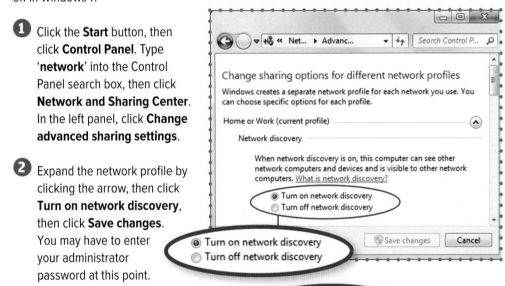

I can't share files on my home network

1 Click the **Start** button, then click **Control Panel**. Type '**network**' into the Control Panel search box, then click **Network and Sharing Center**. In the left panel, click **Change advanced sharing settings**.

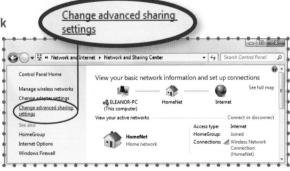

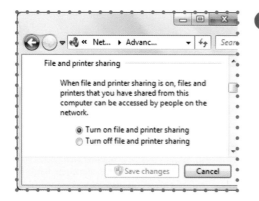

② Expand the network profile by clicking the arrow, then click **Turn on file and printer sharing**, then click **Save changes**. You may have to enter your administrator password at this point.

I want to share files using my Public folders

① Click the **Start** button, then click **Control Panel**. Type 'network' into the Control Panel search box, then click **Network and Sharing Center**. In the left panel, click **Change advanced sharing settings**.

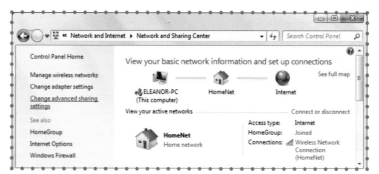

② Expand the network profile by clicking the arrow, then click T**urn on sharing so anyone with network access can read and write files**, then click **Save changes**. You may have to enter your administrator password at this point.

I can't see a shared folder in the computer I'm connecting to
If you can successfully access another computer on your network but
can't see a shared folder, you have to create at least one shared folder
on the computer you are connecting to. Contact the computer's owner
to ensure they can create a shared folder.

How do I create a homegroup in Windows 7?
Windows 7 allows the creation of a special network called a
'homegroup'. This is usually your secure home wireless network and it
allows a high degree of trust between devices on that network, making
it easier to share documents, music and photos.

You need to create a homegroup with a password and then use
this password to give permission to other computers to access your
homegroup. To create a homegroup:

1 Click on the **Start** button
and then click **Control
Panel**. In the Control Panel
window, type '**homegroup**'
into the search box and
in the list of results, click
HomeGroup.

2 Click **Create a
homegroup**, then follow
the instructions on screen.

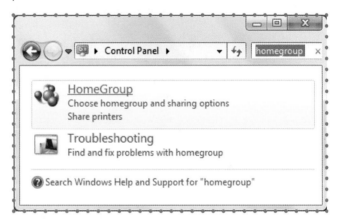

3 If a homegroup has
previously been set up
on your network, then
click **Join now** instead
of Step 2, and follow the
instructions on screen.

▶ Network problems

I CAN'T CONNECT TO THE INTERNET

Not being able to connect to the internet can be very annoying, especially as you can't access help and online forums to solve the problem.

Help! I can't connect to the internet
Try following these simple steps to find and fix the most likely causes:

1 Check all your cables are securely plugged in, such as your modem is connected to a phone socket or your Ethernet cable is securely plugged into both your computer and the router. If in doubt, unplug then plug cables back in.

2 Run the Network troubleshooter to help find and fix any of the more likely problems with Windows 7 or your computer. See page 84 for using the Network troubleshooter.

3 Check your router, especially if it is slightly older. New networking features in Windows 7 can make older routers not work with newer computers. To find out if your router is compatible, download the Internet Connectivity Evaluation Tool from www. microsoft.com/windows/using/tools/igd on another computer, then install it on the computer that can't connect to the internet.

4 Turn off your modem and router, then turn off your computer, and unplug them from the mains, ensuring all lights on the front of the devices go out. Wait 30 seconds, then plug your modem back in and restart it. Plug in the router and restart it. Then plug in the computer and start it. This restart can clear some problems that were affecting the devices.

I can't connect to the internet over my cable or ADSL connection
The vast majority of homes are connected to the internet using a modem that connects to a cable or ADSL broadband. Even if you have a home wireless network, the connection from your modem to the internet is probably wired and either cable or ADSL. Here are some basic checks if things aren't working:

1 Make sure that your cable or ADSL modem is switched on.

2 Check the lights on your modem, as these can highlight a particular problem, such as a lack of connection or lack of power to the modem. Refer to your modem's instruction manual.

3 Ensure the Ethernet cable is plugged in correctly to the modem and the computer. Unplug and restart it again to be sure.

4 Check with your ISP to ensure that its service is running as expected in your area. If it is, check your user account and access details with your ISP to ensure you are using the correct log-on details.

5 A technical problem – called 'Winsock corruption' – can cause internet access problems. To solve it, launch the Network troubleshooter (see page 84 for details on using the Network troubleshooter).

6 Ask your ISP if it uses MAC address filtering. If it does, then you'll need to get your ISP to add the MAC address of your router or modem to its list of devices that can access the network.

Jargon buster

ISP
Your Internet Service Provider is the company that enables and services your connection to the internet.

Jargon buster

Broadband
A method of connecting to the internet via cable or ADSL. It is much faster than a dial-up connection.

I can't connect to the internet using a dial-up modem

While most homes have switched to broadband for internet access, some homes still use a slower dial-up modem that accesses the internet of a standard telephone line. Here are possible solutions to work through if you can't get connected using dial-up.

1 The most common error is not dialling the correct phone number – check the correct number with your ISP.

2 Ensure the phone line and phone socket is working by unplugging the modem and plugging in a working telephone and checking for a dial tone.

TRY THIS

There are many other possible reasons why your setup isn't working. Two good first ports of call are the Microsoft website for Windows-related problems, and the website or tech support line for the manufacturer of your networking kit. Consult them before making too many changes to your system.

3 Check the modem cable that links the modem to the phone socket is working. To test this, plug a working telephone into the 'telephone' socket of your modem, ensure your modem is plugged into a working phone socket, and listen for a dial tone.

4 Turn off your modem and computer and restart after waiting for 30 seconds. Sometimes a dial-up connection is switched off by the ISP if you haven't used it for a period of time. Restarting will turn it back on.

5 Ensure that you have plugged in the phone cable from the phone socket into the 'line' socket of the modem and not into the 'telephone' socket.

6 If you have a call-waiting service from your home phone provider, disable it and try connecting again.

7 Check that someone hasn't used a telephone elsewhere in the home, as doing so can disconnect you from the internet.

I can't connect to the internet wirelessly

Always try connecting via an Ethernet cable first – most routers and computers will support this, and it's quick and easy to do. Not all routers have wireless capability – you may have to buy a new router, or contact your ISP to see if they can offer you an upgrade.

The best place to start with troubleshooting connection problems is Window's Network troubleshooter. It provides you with information about your network connection – for example, it will tell you whether your computer is connected to the router and whether you have access to the internet. See page 84 for help using the Network troubleshooter.

If you've previously been able to connect to the internet wirelessly, resetting the router will often fix the problem. Try turning the router off for 30 seconds and then turning it back on again. Alternatively, right-click on the icon that represents your internet connection in your taskbar and click **Diagnose and Repair**.

Network problems

NETWORK TROUBLESHOOTER

Networks can seem very complicated – and when there's a problem, understandably it can be hard to find the answer. Windows 7 includes a helpful Network troubleshooter than can figure out problems and even repair them.

How can I find the Network troubleshooter?

Windows 7 should automatically give you the option of using the Network troubleshooter when it encounters a networking problem, or you can find it from the Start button or by using the options below.

Error messages If you see a network error message, such as 'Server not available' then the message box should include the option to use the Network troubleshooter. Click the words '**Troubleshoot**' or '**Diagnose**' in an error messages to run the Network troubleshooter.

Notification area Right-click the **Network** icon in the notification area of the taskbar, then choose **Troubleshoot problems** from the pop-up menu.

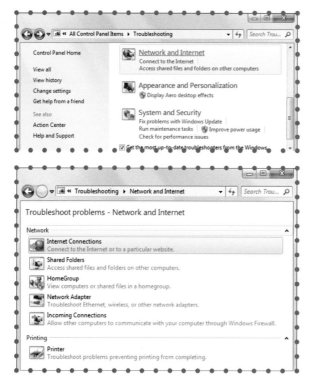

How do I diagnose a network problem?

1 Click the **Start** button, then click **Control Panel**. Type '**troubleshooter**' into the search box of the Control Panel window. Click **Troubleshooting**, then choose option **Network and Internet**.

2 From the list that appears, click the type of problem that you are experiencing. The Network troubleshooter will attempt to figure out the problem.

How do I fix problems with the Network troubleshooter?
The good news is that most basic problems, such as your network connection having been accidently switched off, or your network adapter not waking from sleep, can be fixed by the Network troubleshooter.

If the problem can't be fixed by the Network troubleshooter, it creates a report – called an 'event log' – that details what it found and any technical information. This can be useful if you need to take your computer for repair or call a technical support helpline. To view the event logs:

1 Click the **Start** button, then click **Control Panel**. In the Control Panel window, under **System and Security**, click **Find and fix problems**.

2 Click **View history** in the left pane. Find the event log you are looking for, then right-click it and click **View details**.

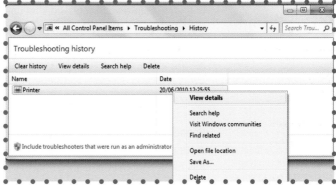

This can be used to help further diagnose a more challenging problem with a networking or computer expert.

85

▶ Network problems

HOW CAN I MAKE MY WEB SURFING FASTER?

Does your broadband connection seem sluggish and slow? If so, try these tips for getting the most from your available online speed.

Change your broadband router

If you access the internet via a wireless network, you may get a slower broadband connection than if connected directly via a router or modem. Connecting via Ethernet or upgrading your wireless broadband router (routers can differ in performance levels and ease of use) could make a real difference to the speed of your connection.

Try the BT Broadband Accelerator

The BT Broadband Accelerator (formerly known as the BT I-Plate) is a self-install device that can be fitted to your main telephone socket. According to BT, it can help increase your broadband speed by up to 1.5 Mbps by reducing interference from your home telephone extension wiring.

The BT Broadband Accelerator is free for BT Total Broadband customers who order it online (though you'll need to pay postage and packing), but non-BT customers can also get the Accelerator for a small fee. It doesn't work on Virgin Media cable phone lines.

Secure your wireless broadband network

If your wireless broadband network isn't secure, your neighbours may be logging on to and sharing your broadband connection. This will decrease your own broadband speeds. Secure your network by using the security settings within your router's browser (see page 73).

Spring clean your web browser

Every time you access a webpage through your web browser, the browser stores or 'caches' it.

Periodically clearing out your browser's cache will help it to function more efficiently and therefore serve up pages faster. Here's how to do this for the browser you are using:

Internet Explorer 8

 From the **Tools** menu, click **Internet Options**.

Jargon buster

Mbps (Megabits per second)
A measure of the speed of data transfer, often used when talking about the speed of broadband.

Jargon buster

Webpage
Each website on the internet usually has more than one page, these are referred to as webpages. Each webpage has a unique address that you type in to go directly to that page.

2 Select the **General** tab.

3 Under **Browsing history** click **Delete browsing history on exit**. Click **OK** to exit.

Firefox

1 From the **Tools** menu, select **Clear Recent History**.

2 From the **Time range to clear** drop-down menu, select the desired range – this could be from 'Today' to just the 'Last Hour'. Alternatively, to clear your entire cache, select **Everything**.

3 Click the down arrow next to **Details** to choose what history elements to clear, then click **Clear Now**.

Safari

1 From the **Safari** menu, select **Empty Cache**.

2 When prompted, click **Empty** to confirm that you want to empty the cache.

TRY THIS

More people attempt to access the internet at certain times of day than at others. Peak internet times include when America wakes up. If you can avoid going online at these busy times, you'll find you experience a faster broadband speed. Evenings tend to be more congested than during the day or night.

TRY THIS

If possible, try to connect your router or ADSL modem to the main telephone socket in your house. Also, if you connect the router or modem directly to a computer, use the shortest cables you can.

TRY THIS

Internet speeds will seem faster if you only do one thing at a time online. The more you try to do online, the longer each individual task is likely to take. For example, if you're downloading a TV show in the background using BBC iPlayer, this may make online speed slower when surfing from one webpage to another webpage.

Network problems

HOW DO I SWITCH BROADBAND PROVIDER?

Before deciding to switch, talk to your current provider. If you switch broadband provider before the end of any minimum contract term, you may have to pay a hefty broadband cancellation fee. As long as you're outside your minimum contract period, however, your broadband provider will be keen to keep your custom and may well offer you a much more attractive deal, meaning that you might not need to switch.

The process you use to switch internet suppliers will vary depending on whether you're just switching broadband or whether you're changing your home phone service at the same time.

Switching between ADSL broadband providers

If you're switching to and from ADSL broadband (broadband via a BT phone line), you'll need to use the MAC (migration authorization code) process. A MAC is a unique code that identifies your broadband line.

1 Ask your existing broadband provider for your broadband MAC. Make sure you stress you're only asking for your MAC and not cancelling your broadband account; some broadband providers will see requesting your MAC as a sign you want to cancel the service, which is bad if you change your mind.

2 Your broadband provider must provide a MAC on request and should send you the MAC within five working days. Your broadband MAC is valid for 30 days from the date it's issued.

3 Give your MAC to the broadband internet provider you want to switch to. They should process your request and give you a transfer date.

4 If you have problems switching between broadband providers because of difficulties obtaining a MAC from your existing broadband supplier, take a look at Ofcom's advice (http://consumers.ofcom.org.uk).

Switching to or from cable broadband

Cable broadband provider Virgin Media does not use the MAC broadband switching process. If you're switching your service to or from Virgin Media, you simply cancel your existing service and sign up to your new broadband service. You may need a new broadband line.

Switching your phone and broadband services simultaneously

If you're switching to or from a provider that offers phone and broadband services bundled together, you may not be able to use the MAC broadband switching process for technical reasons. However, under Ofcom's switching regulations, phone and broadband bundle providers are still required to make the switch as easy for you as possible. You can find detailed advice on the various broadband and phone switching processes on Ofcom's website (www.ofcom.org.uk).

Each of the three processes aims for the minimum possible disruption, though there's a chance you may experience some loss of service. In each case, ask your new supplier which broadband and phone switching process to use and how long the switch will take.

network problems

Network problems

I'VE LOST MY WI-FI PASSWORD

If you want to connect a new device to a home Wi-Fi wireless network, but have forgotten the password to join the network, you'll need to try to recover the password or reset your router with a new password.

1 Check another connected device – such as another computer – to see if you can display the password in its Network settings. In Windows 7:

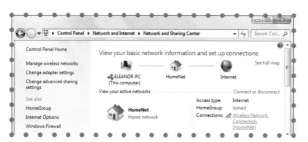

▶ Click the **Start** button, then click **Control Panel**. In the Control Panel window, under **Network and Internet** click **View network status and tasks**. Under the **View your active networks** section, click the name next to **Connections**.

▶ Click **Wireless Properties** in the window that appears, then click the **Security** tab in the new window that appears. Tick the **Show characters** tick box to reveal the password.

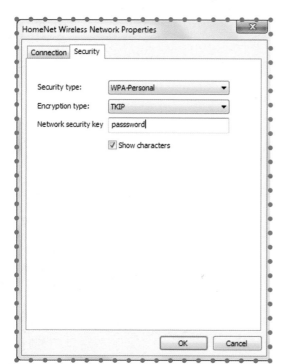

If you still can't see the password, you'll need to reset your router. Refer to your router's manual for specific instructions, but on most routers a small, recessed button should be pressed and held for a time to reset the router back to its original settings.

2 Set up the router and connected devices as detailed in the router's instruction manual.

INTERNET AND EMAIL

By reading and following all the steps in this chapter, you will get to grips with:

- ▶ **Fixing common web browser and Internet Explorer problems**

- ▶ **Making webpages accessible and fixing problems printing webpages**

- ▶ **Fixing email sending problems, and stopping junk email**

MY WEB BROWSER ISN'T WORKING CORRECTLY

If you find that Microsoft Internet Explorer 7 or 8 isn't working correctly, such as it loading websites slowly or not at all, then you can follow a few steps to see if you can improve it.

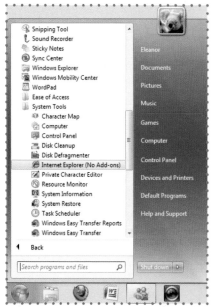

Disable add-ons

Internet Explorer add-ons can add new features to your web browsing, such as viewing 3D websites, but can sometimes cause problems with Internet Explorer. Start Internet Explorer without add-ons to see if it improves things:

1 Click the **Start** button, then click **All Programs**, then click **Accessories**, then click **System Tools**, and finally click **Internet Explorer (No Add-ons)**.

2 If it works, see page 104 for help using the add-on manager to turn individual add-ons on or off until you isolate the problematic add-on.

Run the Microsoft Malicious Software Removal Tool

Another probable cause of Internet Explorer problems is a virus or malicious piece of software causing havoc. For more advice on viruses, see page 124. You can also download and run the Microsoft Malicious Software Removal Tool. Visit www.microsoft.com to download the tool to check your computer for viruses and malicious software.

Reset Internet Explorer

If the problem isn't solved by disabling add-ons or running the Malicious Software Removal Tool, then try resetting Internet Explorer back to its original settings. More detailed help on resetting Internet Explorer is on page 100.

1 If open, close Internet Explorer.

2 Click the **Start** button, then click **Internet Explorer**.

③ Click the **Tools** button, then click **Internet Options**. In the **Advanced** tab, click **Reset**. Then click **Reset** in the message window that appears.

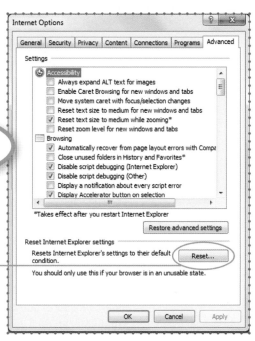

④ Click **Close**, then click **OK**. Close Internet Explorer and restart it as in Step 2. All settings will be returned to the default settings.

Update Internet Explorer

Software updates can fix problems with Internet Explorer, as well as fix potential ways that software can harm or slow down Internet Explorer. Always ensure you are running the latest version of Internet Explorer. For more information on software updates, see page 188.

① Click the **Start** button, then click **Internet Explorer**.

② Click the **Safety** button in Internet Explorer 8, then click **Windows Update**. Follow the instructions on screen to update Internet Explorer.

BE CAREFUL

Resetting Internet Explorer can lead to the permanent loss of information. See page 100 to fully understand what is removed before you reset Internet Explorer.

COMMON WEBSITE ERROR MESSAGES

Surfing the web is usually stress free, but sometimes sites refuse to load or show strange messages on the screen that don't provide much help in telling you what is wrong. Some common website error messages that appear in Internet Explorer 8 are decoded below so you know what the problem is, along with suggested solutions.

The webpage cannot be found (HTTP 400)

What it means There is a problem with the website address, but Internet Explorer is able to connect to the website server.
What you can do Try retyping the website address again after checking it is correct.

The website declined to show this webpage (HTTP 403)

What it means The website can be contacted by Internet Explorer, but Internet Explorer doesn't have permission to show the page.
What you can do If you should have access to the webpage, then contact the website owner to give your web browser permission to view it. If it is a public website, then it may be that the webpage hasn't been set up properly and contains an error that is preventing it from being shown. Alternatively, it may be that the webpage is out of date and no longer exists. Try retyping the web address into Internet Explorer.

The webpage cannot be found (HTTP 404)

What it means The specific webpage cannot be found. This is either usually caused by the page being deleted by the website owner or the page not currently being made available.
What you can do Try again at a later time and check you are typing in the correct web address.

The webpage cannot display the page (HTTP 405)

What it means Internet Explorer is having problems downloading the webpage to your computer.
What you can do Try contacting the website owner to alert them of the problem, as it is usually due to a problem with the webpage itself.

Internet Explorer cannot read this webpage format (HTTP 406)

What it means This is a rare error message. It means that Internet Explorer can download the webpage, but the format is of a kind that it doesn't know how to show or it doesn't understand what format it is.

What you can do If you are trying to view a document, such as a Microsoft Word file, then make sure you have added the correct file extension (such as .doc) to the end of the URL.

The website is too busy to show the webpage (HTTP 408 or 409)
What it means Either the page is very popular and lots of people are trying to look at it at once, leading to a long delay in showing it, or the web server is being slow at showing the page.
What you can do Try accessing the website later at a different time.

The webpage no longer exists (HTTP 410)
What it means Internet Explorer can talk to the website server, but the webpage has permanently been switched off by the website owner.
What you can do Recheck the webpage address and try again or contact the site owner to see if the page has been turned off.

COMMON BROWSER PROBLEMS

When trying to place an order online, I get a security message saying 'The security certificate has expired or is not yet valid'. Is it still safe for me to proceed?

A security certificate contains data that is transferred from one computer to another to prove the authenticity or security of information on the internet. You're probably receiving this message because your computer's date and time are set incorrectly.

If this isn't the case and it is one particular site that you're having problems with, get in touch with them to make sure that the problem isn't with the website itself. When you're making a payment online also remember to check that the web address begins with https:// rather than just http:// and look for the secure padlock icon alongside the address.

When I try to open a webpage, I get the message 'Internet Explorer cannot display the webpage'

First try opening a different page, it may be a problem with the particular website you're trying to look at – the site may be temporarily unavailable or experiencing problems. If you get the same message on other pages, then click on **Diagnose Connection Problem**. This will launch Windows' network diagnostic tool, which will scan for any network problems.

Jargon buster

File extension
The letters that appear after a file name. They show what type of document it is and what type of program will open it – for example, a Microsoft Word document will end in .doc.

Jargon buster

URL
A website's 'address' is called a Uniform Resource Locator.

Sometimes when I'm using the internet, a webpage freezes and I can't click on anything

Unresponsive programs can stop your PC from working. Press **Ctrl+Alt+Delete** and click **Start Task Manager**. A separate window will appear displaying all of your open programs. If one says **Not responding**, click on it and then click **End Task**. If a separate window then pops up, click **End now**. This saves you from having to shut down your computer and restart.

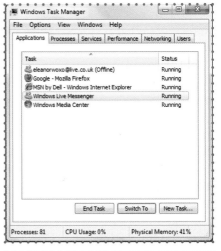

I keep getting lots of pop-up ads when I'm using the internet.
How can I stop them?
Pop-ups can be annoying and confusing; some can even contain malicious code or phishing scams. To block pop-ups in Internet Explorer click **Tools**, then **Internet options**, then select the **Privacy** tab, and make sure that there's a tick next to **Turn on pop-up blocker**.

Often when I open a webpage, I get an ActiveX message at the top of the screen
ActiveX is a legitimate Microsoft technology that enables small programs such as games to be installed via your browser. A message will usually appear near your web browser's toolbar asking if you want to allow the program to be installed. However, ActiveX can install

adware, viruses or harmful Trojans on your computer without your knowledge if you accept an ActiveX control without checking whether it's from a trusted source.

Part of the toolbar on my web browser is missing. How do I get it back?

Right-click on a blank space on the toolbar and make sure there is a tick next to the toolbars that you want to appear at the top of your web browser. You can click on **Customize** to change the layout of icons, or make them bigger.

internet & email

Jargon buster

Adware
Software that tracks your web use to determine your interests and deliver relevant adverts.

Jargon buster

Trojan
A computer virus that disguises itself as an innocent program to entice people to install it. Trojans can allow third parties complete access to your computer remotely.

TRY THIS

If Internet Explorer keeps closing as soon as you open it, you could have low memory on your computer. See page 22 for help on solving memory problems.

RESETTING YOUR HOME PAGE

Your home page is the first webpage you see whenever you open the internet. This is usually set to a default page but you can change this to anything you want such as a particular news site, your webmail service or to keep up to date with a blog.

1 Go to the webpage you'd like to use as your home page.

2 Click the arrow to the right of the **Home** button, and then click **Add or Change Home Page**.

3 Click **Yes** to save your changes.

4 To go to the home page at any time, click the **Home page** icon.

Can I reset my home page?

If you want to restore your home page back to its default setting, you can reset Internet Explorer in Windows 7.

1 Close Internet Explorer if it is running and any Windows Internet Explorer windows.

2 Click the **Start** button, then click **Internet Explorer** to reopen the software. Choose **Tools**, then click **Internet Options**.

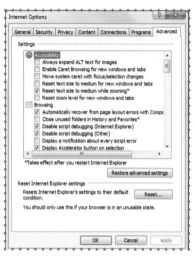

3 Click **Reset** in the **Advanced** tab.

4 Click **Reset** in the **Reset Internet Explorer Settings** message that appears.

5 Once reset, click **Close**, then click **OK**.

I can't change my home page!

Some malicious websites will try to hi-jack your web browser, changing your home page, opening lots of windows and preventing you from changing your home page back. Browser hi-jacking is a common event and here is how you stop it:

1 Download the Malicious Software Removal Tool from Microsoft at www.microsoft.com/security/malwareremove/default.aspx.

2 Run the Malicious Software Removal Tool, following the onscreen instructions. This will remove the small program that is 'hi-jacking' your web browser.

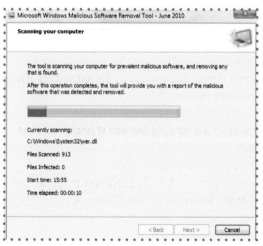

3 Reset your home page as in the steps above.

▶ Internet & email

RESETTING BROWSER SETTINGS

If you are experiencing problems with Internet Explorer – the default web browser in Windows 7 – it can be a good idea to reset it. This returns the browser to its default settings and can solve lots of problems, but it is worth understanding what reset options there are and what actually gets deleted when you reset the browser.

BE CAREFUL

When you reset Internet Explorer back to its factory settings, the reset can't be undone, so make sure you really want to reset Internet Explorer before you do so.

Settings that are permanently deleted when reset
▶ InPrivate Filtering information
▶ Web browsing history, such as the list of recent websites you have visited
▶ Cookies, temporary internet files and any stored passwords
▶ Menu extensions and typed-in web addresses
▶ Websites that you have added to trusted or restricted zones
▶ Websites you have allowed to show pop-up windows

Settings that are saved and not deleted when reset
▶ The Favorites list of your bookmarked websites
▶ Internet applications, such as MSN Messenger
▶ Internet connection settings
▶ The default web browser setting
▶ Pre-approved ActiveX controls
▶ Certificate information, such as a certificate used by your banking site
▶ Any Content Advisor settings used to filter inappropriate websites

Settings that are returned to their original settings when reset
▶ The search box will be restored to the original search engine
▶ Page set-up, toolbar and text size settings
▶ The home page – the first webpage you see when you launch Internet Explorer – will be returned to its original location, such as microsoft.com
▶ Colours, fonts, accessibility and font settings
▶ Most tab settings, such as Privacy and Advanced tab settings
▶ Any settings for the pop-up blocker, zoom settings and AutoComplete settings – when Internet Explorer will automatically fill in web forms based on stored information about you.

Reset Internet Explorer

If you're happy with what will change, then reset Internet Explorer:

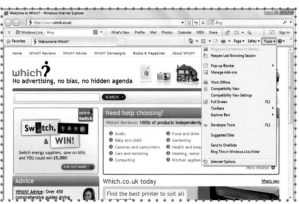

1 If open, close Internet Explorer.

2 Click the **Start** button, then click **Internet Explorer.** Click the **Tools** button, then click **Internet Options**.

3 In the **Advanced** tab, click **Reset**.

4 Tick **Delete personal settings** if you want to remove items, such as browsing history, search providers, home pages and InPrivate Filtering information. Then click **Reset**.

5 Click **Close**, then click **OK**. Close Internet Explorer and restart it as in Step 2. All settings will be returned to the default settings.

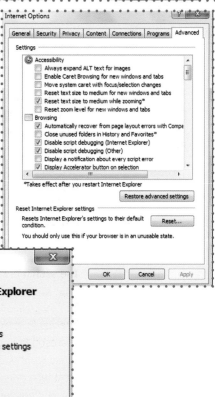

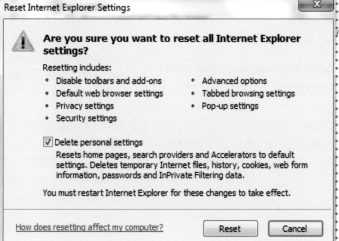

Reset Internet Explorer Settings

Are you sure you want to reset all Internet Explorer settings?

Resetting includes:

- Disable toolbars and add-ons
- Advanced options
- Default web browser settings
- Tabbed browsing settings
- Privacy settings
- Pop-up settings
- Security settings

☑ Delete personal settings
Resets home pages, search providers and Accelerators to default settings. Deletes temporary Internet files, history, cookies, web form information, passwords and InPrivate Filtering data.

You must restart Internet Explorer for these changes to take effect.

How does resetting affect my computer?   Reset   Cancel

REMOVING BROWSER TOOLBARS

Toolbars can be downloaded and added to Internet Explorer to add functionality, such as different page formatting tools. But some toolbars sneakily install themselves without you realizing, or you may simply not like a toolbar any more and want to remove it.

1 Click the **Start** button, then click **Internet Explorer**. Click **Tools**, then click **Manage Add-ons**.

2 Click **Toolbars and Extensions** in the window that appears. In the list of toolbars and add-ons that appear in the central pane, click to select a toolbar.

3 Click **Disable** at the bottom of the window. The toolbar will be removed from Internet Explorer. Repeat the first three steps for each toolbar that you want to remove.

④ Click the **Start** button, then click **Control Panel**, and click **Uninstall a program**. In the search box, type the name of the toolbar you want to remove. Click on the toolbar, then click **Uninstall** to delete the toolbar from your computer.

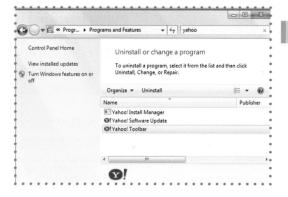

As some toolbars are the result of more malicious programs that sneak onto your computer and even some kinds of malware, it's worth scanning your computer for viruses and spyware at this stage. See page 124 for help in checking if your PC has a virus.

HOW TO BACK UP YOUR HOME PAGE

The home page is the first website or webpage that you see when you first start your web browser such as Internet Explorer. If you need to reinstall or reset Internet Explorer, you will lose your home page settings, but it is possible to back them up so that you can add them back at a later date if you lose them. The best way to save your home page is as a Favourite:

① Click the **Start** button, then click **Internet Explorer**. Let Internet Explorer open and load the home page you want to back up.

② Click and drag the icon in the address bar to the desktop to save it as a file. If you can't see the desktop, click and drag the right-hand corner of the Internet Explorer window towards the centre of the screen to reveal the desktop, then click and drag the icon.

③ To restore this as a home page, double-click the icon on the desktop to launch the webpage, then set it as a home page according to 'Resetting your home page' on page 98.

Internet & email

INTERNET EXPLORER ADD-ON PROBLEMS

Add-ons are small programs that add extra features and functionality to Internet Explorer in Windows 7. They can add extra toolbars, block pop-up ads, and add news tickers to Internet Explorer – but some can also cause problems.

Checking the Add-ons you have installed

1 Click the **Start** button, then click **Internet Explorer**. In Internet Explorer, click the **Tools** button, then click **Manage Add-ons**.

2 Under **Add-on Types**, click **Toolbars and Extensions**. You can then see the range of different add-ons used by Internet Explorer.

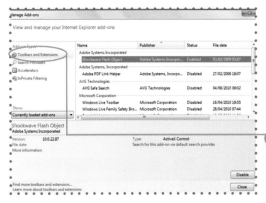

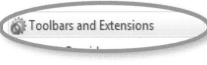

I think an add-on is causing a problem

If Internet Explorer is crashing and shutting down unexpectedly, it is possible that a recently installed add-on is the culprit. To find out, you should run Internet Explorer without add-ons and, if it works fine, test each add-on to isolate the problem.

1 To run Internet Explorer without loading any add-ons, click the **Start** button, then click **All Programs**, then click **Accessories**, then click **System Tools** and then click **Internet Explorer (No Add-ons)**.

If this solves the problem, then open Internet Explorer and do the following:

1 Click the **Tools** button and click **Manage Add-ons**. Click **All Add-ons** under **Show**.

2 Click the Add-on you want to disable, then click **Disable**. Repeat these two steps for each add-on you want to disable. Click **Close** when done.

If you have disabled several add-ons, but need to reactivate a few of them that aren't causing any problems:

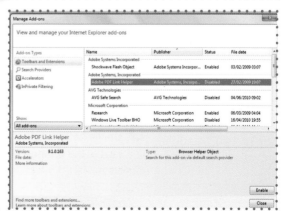

1 Click the **Start** button, then click **Internet Explorer.** In Internet Explorer, click the **Tools** button, then click **Manage Add-ons**.

2 Click **All add-ons** under **Show**.

3 Click the Add-on you want to reactivate, then click **Enable**. Repeat this process for each add-on you want to reactivate. Click **Close** once done.

HOW TO MAKE WEBPAGES MORE ACCESSIBLE

Internet Explorer 8 has several accessibility options that can help make webpages easier to read.

Change webpage text size

1 In Internet Explorer, click the **Page** button, then click **Text Size**.

2 Click the size you want.

Make webpages larger

Internet Explorer Zoom lets you enlarge or reduce the view of a webpage. Unlike changing font size, zoom enlarges or reduces everything on the page, including text and images. You can zoom from 10% to 1,000% in several ways:

1 On the bottom right of the Internet Explorer screen, click the arrow next to the **Change Zoom Level** button.

2 To go to a pre-defined zoom level, click the percentage of enlargement or reduction you want. Holding down the button will cycle through 100%, 125% and 150%, giving you a quick enlargement of the webpage.

3 To specify a zoom level, click **Custom**. In the **Percentage zoom** box, type a zoom value, and then click **OK**.

4 If you have a mouse with a wheel, hold down the **CTRL** key, and then scroll the wheel to zoom in or out (up for in and down for out).

5 From the keyboard you can increase or decrease the zoom value in 10% increments. To zoom in, press **CTRL + PLUS SIGN (+)**. To zoom out, press **CTRL + MINUS SIGN (-)**. To restore the zoom to 100%, press **CTRL + 0**.

I CAN'T FIND THE WEBPAGE I WANT

If you're not sure of a website's exact address or you want to find information on a specific topic, you can use a search engine. The most popular search engine is Google (www.google.co.uk), but Yahoo (www.yahoo.com) and Microsoft's search engine (www.bing.com) are good alternatives. Type one of these addresses into the address bar to take you to its home page from where you can start your search.

Alternatively, the latest versions of web browsers Internet Explorer or Firefox have an instant search box located to the side of the address bar. You can type what you're looking for straight into this box and press **Enter**.

1 Click once in the **Search** box in the top, right-hand corner of the toolbar.

2 Type what you're looking for and press **Enter**.

3 Results will then be displayed on screen.

4 If you can't see what you're looking for, click **Next** at the bottom of the page to see more search results.

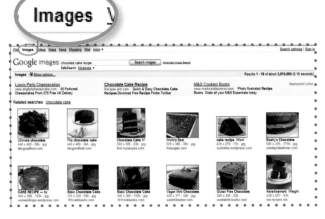

Search engines automatically search for text results first but you can also search for images and video. To search for an image, simply type what you're looking for into the search box and click on the relevant link or button (usually labelled '**Images**') on the search engine's page and press **Enter**.

In addition to Web and Images, Google also offers the search categories News, which search for news-related stories and Shopping, which looks for items for sale for whatever search term you've entered into the search box.

Add another search engine box

If you don't want to use the default search engine that appears on your web browser, you can switch to a different search engine or add a specialist search engine box, for example, an eBay box, which will just search within the eBay site.

1 In Internet Explorer 8 click the arrow to the right of the magnifying glass icon and click **Find More Providers**.

2 You'll see a list of options. Choose the one you want and click **Add to Internet Explorer**. Or you can click **Create your own Search Provider** if you can't see the one you want in the list of options.

3 When you want to switch to a different search engine box, click the arrow next to the magnifying glass to show the list. Click on the search engine you want to use. Then in the box enter the word/s you want to search for and press **Enter**.

SEARCH TIPS

▶ Search engines don't worry about words such as 'the' or 'a', so you don't need to include these in your search terms.

▶ Be specific in your search. If broad search words such as 'car sales' yield too many results, try more specific words such as 'used car classifieds', 'used Honda car sales', or 'London used car classifieds'.

▶ Using punctuation in your searches will make them more efficient. If you're looking for information on the TV show Antiques Roadshow, type "Antiques Roadshow" or either of the words separately.

internet & email

109

PRINTING WEBPAGES

More often than not, printing a webpage results in something that doesn't look anything like it does on the screen. Some common webpage printing problems are tackled below.

Why is the text too small when I print?

In Windows 7, Internet Explorer will automatically shrink text so that it fits the width of the paper, such as A4, that you are printing to. If you're trying to print an unusually wide webpage, the text will be tiny when printed. To avoid shrunk text:

1 Click the arrow next to the Print button in Internet Explorer, then click **Page setup**.

2 Choose a new paper size from the **Page size** drop-down, and change the margins to fit. Change to **Landscape** to print a wide page and untick the **Enable Shrink-to-Fit** option.

This will print a zoomed portion of the webpage, but some information may be cut off.

Alternatively, you can copy and paste sections of the webpage into a word processor such as Microsoft Word and print them separately.

Why is the printed webpage a mess?

This may be due to background images and colours stopping you from reading the text. To turn this off in Internet Explorer 8:

1 Click the arrow next to the Print button in Internet Explorer, then click **Page setup**.

2 Untick the **Print Background Colors and Images** tick box, then click **OK**.

Why are parts of a webpage not printing?

While the text and images from a webpage will print fine, some elements won't print out at all, such as Adobe Flash presentations. To print this type of content:

1 Right-click the Flash content on the webpage.

2 Choose **Print** from the pop-up menu. This content will then print normally.

Jargon buster

Flash content
A type of interactive content, such as an animated cartoon. Interactive, animated parts of a web page such as a game, animation or interactive presentation is usually created in a format called 'Flash'.

My printer won't print webpages at all

Web browsers work with your printer in the same way as any program on your computer, so if you can't print a webpage at all, then there may be a problem with your printer, or the print settings in Windows 7. See page 68 for information on solving printer problems.

HOW TO MAKE SURFING SAFE FOR KIDS

If you're a parent and allow your children to use your computer to access the internet, maybe for homework or to communicate with friends, you'll be aware that the internet is also full of potential dangers and inappropriate material that you might not want your children exposed to. With some simple changes, it is possible to make the internet seen by your children appropriate for their age and maturity.

Setting up parental controls

Windows 7 uses Parental Controls to manage how children access the internet and programs on your computer, such as age-restricted games. You will need to be logged on as an administrator to set up Parental Controls. See page 29 for more information on this.

1 Click the **Start** button, then click **Control Panel**, then in **User Accounts and Family Safety**, click **Set up parental controls for any user**. You may need to enter your administrator password at this stage.

2 Click the account name that you want to apply parental controls to. This should be the account that your child or children use to log on to the computer. See page 28 for help with accounts.

3 Adjust the individual settings as required for the account:

▶ **Time Limits** This controls when that account can log on to the computer, and stops a child logging on outside of the hours you set. It's possible to set different times for different days of the week. If they are logged on when their time limit expires, they will be automatically logged off.

▶ **Game Ratings** This controls the age-rating of different types of games and whether to block unrated or specific games.

▶ **Allow and block specific programs** This handy setting lets you determine which programs children can load and use.

To determine when children can use the computer

1 Click the **Start** button, then click **Control Panel**, then under **User Accounts and Family Safety**, click **Set up parental controls for any user**. You may need to enter your administrator password at this stage.

2 Click the account name that you want to apply parental controls to. Click **On, enforce current settings**.

3 Click **Time Limits**. In the grid that appears, click and drag the hours that you want to block or allow. Click **OK**.

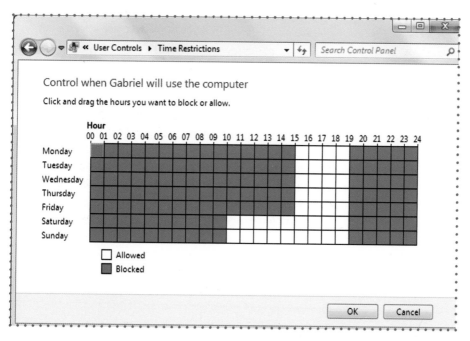

Limit what children can see on the web

As well as setting general rules around when children can use your computer and what they can use when they are logged on, it's possible to restrict what they can and cannot access when surfing the web. You can allow or block specific websites using the Parental Control settings.

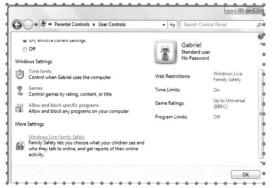

① Click the **Start** button, then click **Control Panel**, then under **User Accounts and Family Safety,** click **Set up parental controls for any user.** You may need to enter your administrator password at this stage.

② Click the account name that you want to apply parental controls to. Click **On, enforce current settings**.

③ Click **Windows Live Family Safety** (download details are on page 209) to run it and choose an account to manage. You will need a Window Live ID for this. You will be prompted if you don't have one – follow the instructions to get an ID.

④ Click **Web filtering**, then move the slider to the appropriate setting for your child. Click **Save** to save your changes.

Top tips on managing your child's online activities

When children are using the internet, it's advisable to keep the computer in a family place like the living room. That way, being online becomes a social, family activity. However, in reality, it's impossible to keep an eye on the screen at all times.

Child safety/parental control software can help you manage your child's computer use and internet access in a way that's appropriate to their age.

Parental control software isn't for everyone, and will never be a substitute for educating children about online dangers and keeping an open communication with your child. But having an extra line of defence can make a big difference.

Blocking programs

Some software can be set up to prevent children from running programs you don't want them to, including games, chat programs or file-sharing tools. It can also prevent personal details, such as a telephone number, from being typed out, block any emails sent to unfamiliar people or disallow chat messages to strangers.

Another useful tool is the ability to track or monitor your child's internet activity. Logs of websites they've visited, the times they've spent online and, in some cases, transcripts of chat conversations, can all be viewed in report form.

▶ When you first install parental control software, you'll need to set up a master password to let you access and configure any settings. This password will also be required to uninstall the software.

▶ Most will also analyse websites on the fly and block them if they're deemed inappropriate – they will detect the presence of certain words, for example.

▶ Whenever the software blocks a website, an alert should appear on screen. If the site has been incorrectly blocked and your child legitimately wishes to access the site, they can ask you to enter your master password to unblock it.

▶ You can also control the applications your child is allowed to use and set the hours they are allowed to use the computer. For very young children, you may only want to introduce them to a select few chosen websites. You can add pre-approved websites to a 'whitelist', and prevent your children from accessing those that are not on the approved list.

TIP
You can prevent file downloads by selecting the **Block file downloads** tick box.

TRY THIS
Parental controls work in a similar way to anti-virus and anti-spam software. They will often 'blacklist' sites known to be questionable, such as those related to pornography, hate speech, gambling or drugs.

Internet & email

WHY CAN'T I SEE A WEBPAGE PROPERLY?

Some websites have been designed to be displayed in older versions of Internet Explorer, which means that they may not show properly when using Internet Explorer in Windows 7.

Webpage viewing problems can be caused by lots of factors, such as slow bandwidth and problems with the webpage code used on the website that can stop it working properly.

I can't see the webpage properly

You can use the Compatibility View option to make an older webpage look better in Windows 7 running Internet Explorer:

1 Click the **Start** button, then click **Internet Explorer**.

2 When Internet Explorer opens, click the **Tools** button, then click **Compatibility View**.

When switched on, a Compatibility View button will appear in the toolbar of Internet Explorer when it visits a webpage that isn't compatible. If pressed, it will reshow the page as if you were using an older version of Internet Explorer.

I can't see the images on a webpage

If when you visit a webpage you are faced with a series of bordered boxes with red crosses in the middle, it means the web browser is unable to show the images on the page. Check first that Internet Explorer is set up to show images:

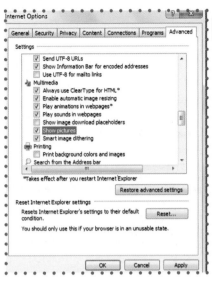

1. Click the **Start** button, then click **Internet Explorer**. When Internet Explorer opens, click the **Tools** button, then click **Internet Options**, and then the **Advanced** tab.

2. Tick the **Show Pictures** option under the **Multimedia** section, then click **OK**.

If you still can't see any images, it may be that you don't have enough space to download the images within Internet Explorer. To fix this you'll need to clear the cache:

1. Click the **Start** button, then click **Internet Explorer**.

2. When Internet Explorer opens, click the **Safety** button, then click **Delete Browsing History**.

3. To keep cookies and files that are associated with your Favorites websites, tick the **Preserve Favorites website data** tick box. Tick each box next to the category of files that you want to delete. Click **Delete**, then click **OK**.

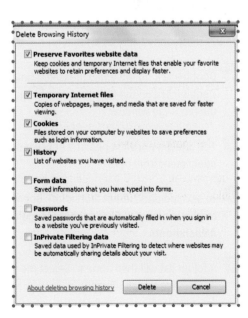

Jargon buster

Cookie
A piece of information sent to a user's web browser by a website. The web browser then returns that information to the website. This is how some websites 'remember' your previous visits.

ATTACHMENTS TO EMAILS

Sometimes you might want to send a picture or separate document with your email. Here's how to do it:

Attach a file to an email

1 Once you've written your email, click the **paper clip** icon.

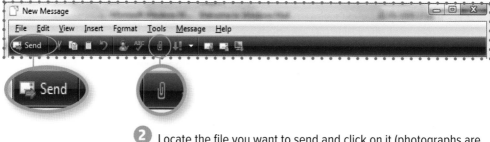

2 Locate the file you want to send and click on it (photographs are probably in your Pictures folder).

3 Click **Open**.

4 The file will appear in the **Attach** box.

5 You can add more attachments in the same way. When you have attached them all, click **Send**.

Open an attachment in an email you have been sent

1 Double-click on the email message that contains the attachment. Double-click on the file attachment icon that appears at the top of the message window.

2 The attachment will open in a new window. You can save the attachment from here.

3 To save an attachment first before opening it, open the message as above and click **File** in the message window. Click **Save Attachments**.

4 A folder list will then appear. Select the folder into which you'd like to save the attachment.

BE CAREFUL

Attaching files and pictures to your emails can create unwieldy emails – if your email attachment is too big, you may see an error message that means it exceeds the email attachment limit for your account.

BE CAREFUL

Only open attachments if you know the sender. Those from unknown senders could contain viruses. See page 124 for more on computer security.

HOW TO ATTACH A PHOTO TO YOUR EMAIL

Digital cameras can generate very large image files that may clog up another person's inbox if you attach them to an email. The size might even mean the image gets sent to the recipient's junk mail folder or is blocked altogether. Windows 7, however, has a tool that lets you resize pictures for easy emailing. Consider what the recipient wants to do with it before choosing an image size (see point 4).

1 Click the **Start** button.

2 Click **All Programs**, then click **Windows Live**, then click **Windows Live Photo Gallery**.

3 Click on the picture you want to email. Click **E-mail** at the top of the window.

TRY THIS

In many email programs you can right-click on an attachment and click **Properties** to see more information about it, including size and file type.

4 Choose a size from the drop-down menu. For viewing photos on screen the 'smaller' size is fine. This size will be suitable for printing photos at 4 × 6 inches. Both 'medium' and 'large' are suitable for printing photos sized 5 × 7 inches.

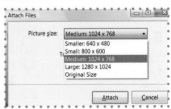

5 You'll then see the estimated size of your attachment. Anything less than 1 MB is fine to send via email. If it's OK, click **Attach**.

Internet & email

HOW DO I STOP JUNK EMAIL?

The electronic equivalent of junk mail, spam can clog up your inbox. Spam emails may also contain offensive material and can be carriers of viruses and phishing scams (see page 96).

Your ISP will use spam filters on their email server in an attempt to prevent spam from reaching your inbox, and webmail accounts usually feature spam filters too. You can also change your email program's junk email settings to filter out certain types of message automatically.

Filter junk mail in Windows Live Mail (Hotmail)

1 With your Windows Live Mail account open, click **Options** at the top right of your screen. Click **More options**.

2 Under **Junk Mail**, click **Filters and Reporting**.

3 From the list that appears, you can select how your account deals with junk mail. Click **Save** at the bottom of the page when you've made your choice.

Filter junk mail in Windows Mail

1 With your Windows Mail account open, click **Tools** on the toolbar.

2 Click **Junk E-mail Options**. A window will appear. Here you can choose the level of protection you want.

3 Make your choices and click **Apply**. Click **OK**.

TIPS FOR AVOIDING JUNK EMAIL

Don't reply to spam emails

Replying to spam emails or clicking on an 'unsubscribe' link within them confirms to the sender that your email address is genuine. Delete them without opening the message.

Create a 'disposable' email address

Create a separate email to use for online shopping, forums and signing up for services – something like a free Windows Live Hotmail account (http://mail.live.com) that you can always scrap and start again.

Choose a complicated email address

Picking an obscure email address can help prevent spammers from sending anything to you.

Use a spam filter

It is best to keep the junk at bay by using a dedicated spam filter. The best filters use a whitelist for 'good' email addresses and a blacklist for addresses, keywords and phrases that you don't want in your inbox. Most email accounts include a spam filter, but there are also dedicated spam-filtering tools available, including free downloadable ones like Mailwasher (www.mailwasher.net) and SpamFighter (www.spamfighter.com).

Identify spam to your email provider

Report spam to your internet service provider or webmail service provider. This can help your provider to determine and eliminate future spam emails. Often you can do this by clicking **Report this email as junk** when prompted.

BE CAREFUL

Never reply to spam emails or click on an 'unsubscribe' link within them as this confirms that your email address is genuine. Simply delete them without opening the message.

HOW CAN I STOP MY EMAILS BOUNCING BACK?

If you've spent ages writing an email and then sending it, but it is returned with an error that it can't be delivered, the email has 'bounced back'. Here are some tips for reducing email bounce backs.

Are you typing the correct email address?

Most emails follow the email convention of name@somewhere, such as mrsmith@which.co.uk where the name is the email name, and the somewhere is the location or domain. Make sure you are typing in the correct email address.

Does the email address exist?

If it is returned quickly, then probably not. Check with the person you are sending the email to that you have their correct email address.

Have you attached too big a file?

Some email accounts, such as business email addresses, have a limit on the file size of any attachments with the email. Usually, this is around 10 MB. Try sending the email without the attachment to see if it gets through.

Your email has a problem with the attachment

Some email programs and services, such as Gmail, won't allow certain types of attachments – such as executable programs – to be received on their network due to the likelihood they are malware. Additionally, your attachment may have been infected by a virus, which means the email service won't deliver it to the address. For help checking for viruses, see page 124.

SECURITY PROBLEMS

By reading and following all the steps in this chapter, you will get to grips with:

- ▶ **How to check your computer for viruses and spyware and remove them**

- ▶ **How to be confident when visiting websites**

- ▶ **Setting up and managing a firewall to protect your computer**

HOW TO CHECK A PC FOR A VIRUS

Short of running an anti-virus scan using your security software, how can you tell if your computer may be infected by a virus? Malware – of which a virus is one type – often has some telltale symptoms that could mean you have a virus infection.

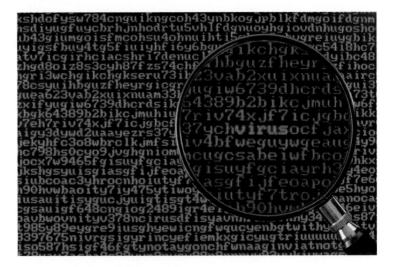

Has the computer slowed down significantly?
If your computer is slowing down when performing tasks, and is significantly slower than it should be, this can be an indication that you have a virus.

Have strange toolbars, home pages or links appeared?
This is a good indication that you have been infected by spyware – a kind of software that is designed to watch and record your activity when using your computer, such as keystrokes used to enter banking passwords – and then pass them onto criminals.

Are programs starting automatically or crashing repeatedly?
Some viruses are designed to sabotage programs, making them run in strange ways, automatically start without you asking or refusing to run and crashing.

Is there a lot of activity on your network?
Telltale signs include your modem or hard disk working all the time or if the activity lights on your broadband modem are constantly lit. This doesn't automatically mean you have a virus, but when combined with other symptoms it is a possible indicator.

Have you recently downloaded a program from the web?
While many programs are perfectly safe to download, some programs – usually free screensavers, games and animated cursors – can contain hidden viruses or spyware. If you noticed a change after downloading and installing software, then use a previous restore point to return your computer back to a time before you installed it. See page 180 for help on using restore points.

What to do to scan for viruses and spyware
Make sure you have adequate security software and scan for viruses. Each software package is different, so follow the instructions for scanning the computer that came with the software. There will probably be a large Scan button – it can take a while to scan a computer with a large hard drive for viruses.

There are lots of commercial security software suites available for protecting your computer from viruses and spyware, and many free software solutions that protect against viruses. Commercial packages include Symantec Norton Internet Security and Kaspersky Internet Security. Free packages include AVG Anti-Virus Free and Windows Defender, which is installed in Windows 7 and will scan and remove spyware.

security problems

Jargon buster

Hard disk
The main long-term storage space used by your computer to store data. Also known as a hard drive.

⏵ Security problems

HELP! I HAVE A VIRUS

The new, free AVG 9.0 software from Grisoft includes basic, yet effective, anti-virus and anti-spyware tools. Previous versions have earned Best Buy status on Which? Computing security tests. Because AVG doesn't cost a penny, it is only meant for personal use and there is no formal technical support. But it's easy to install and use.

1 Download the installation file. It's a little tricky to find where the free version (AVG 9.0) is on the Grisoft website. Make sure you aren't incorrectly downloading a trial version of their fully featured software that you'll need to pay for later.

Enter **http://free.grisoft.com** into the address bar of your web browser, and click **Get it now** in the section where it says AVG

Anti-Virus Free Edition – this is the version you'll need. Next, click the link that says **Download** under the column headed **AVG Anti-Virus Free Edition**.

On the following page, click the left-hand column that is headed **Get AVG Anti-Virus Free Edition 9.0**. Clicking this will take you to the CNet Download.com partner site. Once there, click **Download Now** and the file should save to your desktop.

2 Install the program. Close all open applications and then

double-click the **AVG file** you just downloaded (it will be located in your Downloads folder) to start installing it by pressing **Run**. For security reasons, you may receive a warning at this point (or you may need to use your computer's administrator username and password) but it's safe to continue. To install the program, follow the easy steps, choosing **Install only basic free protection** when you're asked to choose an installation type. Once done, click **Next** and the remainder of the software will download from the internet and install.

Towards the end of the process, you can, if you wish, choose not to add the AVG Security Toolbar to your web browser by unticking the box (most browsers have a similar toolbar built in so it's safe to omit this feature). At the end of the installation process click **OK**.

3 Configure the software. Once AVG has successfully installed, choose **Optimize scanning now** (recommended) as this will speed up future scans. Once finished, **launch AVG Free 9.0** from the **Start** menu, choosing **AVG Free User Interface**. The main interface will launch and everything should have a green tick and a reassuring **You are protected** message in green.

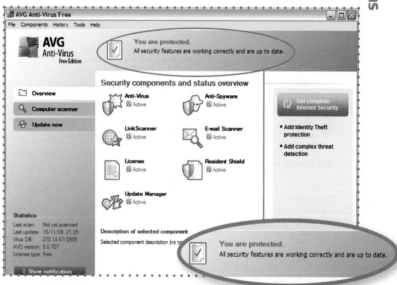

4 Click the **Computer scanner** tab, then **Scan whole computer**. This will examine the entire computer hard drive to check for any resident viruses or spyware – be aware that this scan can take a while to run. If it finds any infected files, AVG will remove and repair them.

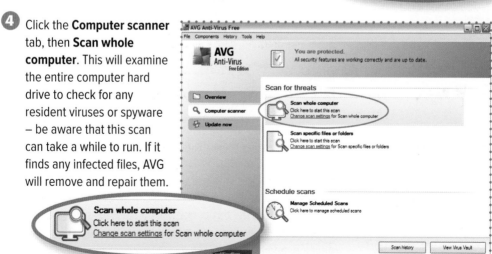

⑤ To schedule scans, click the **Computer scanner** tab and then click **Manage Scheduled Scans**. The screen that appears shows a list of scheduled scans. To change timings, click the **Edit scan schedule** button. Tick the **Enable this task** option. In the **Schedule running** section, choose a time interval, such as **Run at a specific time interval**. The default is midday once per week. Tick **Run on computer startup if task has been missed**.

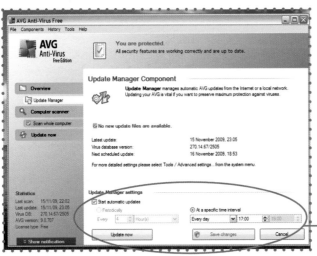

⑥ To update software, AVG will automatically update at least once a day to keep you protected from the latest threats. To change the default, double-click **Update Manager** from the **Overview** tab. Ensure **Start automatic updates** is ticked, and set a time, such as 5pm every day.

⑦ In order to keep your PC protected every day from now on, AVG will automatically do an update and scan your PC once a week. Because you've downloaded a free version, AVG will occasionally encourage you to upgrade to a more complete version, but this won't be free. You can ignore these messages – we found that the basic, free version of AVG, combined with the other security software elements mentioned earlier, does an effective enough job.

HOW TO REMOVE SPYWARE

Windows Defender is a software product that detects, removes or quarantines spyware. The product is installed and enabled by default in Windows 7.

Where to find Windows Defender on your PC

To access Windows Defender from Windows, click the **Start** button, point to **Control Panel** and then click **System and Security**. Type '**windows defender**' into the search box, then click **Windows Defender** in the list of results.

Performing a manual scan

1 Click **Scan** and Defender will look for spyware. The scan may take a few minutes. You can then ignore, remove or quarantine files.

Setting up an automatic scan

1 To set your computer to run an automatic, daily scan, click **Tools** then **Options**.

2 Using the drop-down arrows, select a daily scan and your preferred time for the scan to run.

3 You can also tell Defender what to do when it finds, for instance, high alert items, again by using the drop-down menus.

4 Click **Save and Continue**.

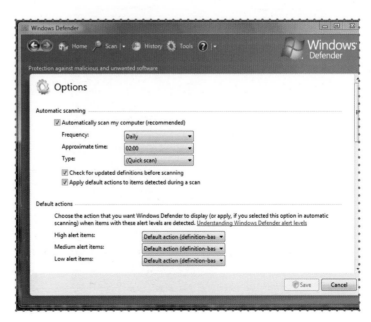

HOW TO STOP VIRUSES

Protecting your computer from viruses and other threats isn't difficult, but you have to be diligent.

Install an anti-virus program

Ideally, you should have anti-virus software to scan for, block and remove viruses. You should also have a firewall to block unauthorized traffic to and from the internet on your computer (see page 134 on setting up Windows Firewall).

Installing an anti-virus program and keeping it up to date can help defend your computer against viruses. Anti-virus programs scan for viruses trying to get into your email, operating system or files. New viruses appear daily, so check the anti-virus manufacturer's website frequently for updates. Most anti-virus programs are sold with annual subscriptions, which can be renewed as needed.

Think twice about opening email attachments

If you get an email with an attachment, such as a photo or program, that you were not expecting, then think twice before opening it. Many viruses are spread by email attachments and will infect your computer when you open the attachment.

Keep Windows 7 updated

Hackers are always trying to find holes in the security in Windows 7 so they can attack computers running the system. Microsoft regularly releases security updates in an on-going game of cat and mouse with the hackers. It's important to ensure Windows 7 is up to date. To do this automatically, see page 184.

Make sure your firewall is turned on

A good way of stopping malware and viruses dead in their tracks is to ensure that Windows Firewall is turned on properly in Windows 7. A firewall protects your files and blocks hackers from accessing your PC and downloading valuable information. See page 134 for details on turning on Windows Firewall.

▶ Security problems

HOW CAN I BE SURE OF A WEBSITE?

The internet is all about sharing. From email messages, opinions, comments and recommendations to photos, video and music – the internet lets us share information and content with others around the world. You can find information on just about every topic imaginable – but how can you be sure that what you're reading is accurate and genuine?

Anyone can publish anything on the web, and it can be hard to determine first a webpage's author and second their knowledge and qualifications on a given subject. It's also difficult to decide whether a webpage is a mask for advertising or product sponsorship, or is simply biased in some way.

To help decide if information on a website can be trusted, consider the following:

Accuracy
Is it clear who is the website author: an individual or a company/institution? Is there an About button or contact details for those responsible for the site?

Authority
Does the webpage list the author and company/institution credentials? Look at the site's web address. Domains ending in .edu and .gov are for educational and government sites only, while domains ending .org and .net are mainly used for non-profit organizations, such as charities.

Objectivity
Does the website clearly state its objectives? Does it promote just one point of view, product or service? If it has any advertising support, is it obvious?

Currency
Is the webpage current and updated regularly? Some website information can be very out of date. Check that links to other sites (if it has any) work, as out-of-date links are often a sign that a webpage is rarely updated.

Coverage

Can you view the information you need fully or are you limited by payment requests, browser technology or software requirements?

If you can answer yes to all or most of the above, you will able to decide if a website is trustworthy in the information it provides.

How can I be sure a website is secure?

A secure website will be prefaced https:// rather than the usual http:// – the extra 's' standing for 'secure'. In Internet Explorer and Firefox, a padlock icon also appears in the address bar every time you arrive at a secure page. You can check the security certificate for a webpage to make sure it's genuine too.

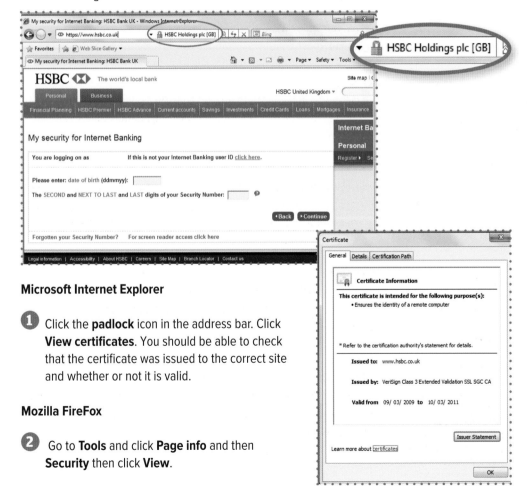

Microsoft Internet Explorer

1 Click the **padlock** icon in the address bar. Click **View certificates**. You should be able to check that the certificate was issued to the correct site and whether or not it is valid.

Mozilla FireFox

2 Go to **Tools** and click **Page info** and then **Security** then click **View**.

Security problems

TRY THIS

If you want to block all communications through the firewall from your computer, choose **Block all incoming connections**, including those in the list of allowed programs option. While this is an option, many programs do need to communicate through a firewall and this setting may stop them working properly.

SETTING UP A FIREWALL

A firewall sounds scary – but it's a vital part of Windows 7, and can help stop malware and even hackers from breaking into your computer over a network. It works by monitoring files going to and fro from your computer and blocks any potential threats before they get onto your computer. Think of it as a wall of fire around your valuable data that can open to let good files through but blocks off threats.

If your firewall isn't turned on, your computer is at real risk of being compromised – leading to poor performance and potential loss of data. Windows 7 allows you to set different levels of firewall protection depending on your location – such as lower settings at home and tougher settings when using a computer such as a laptop in public.

I think my firewall isn't turned on

By default, most Windows 7 computers will have the Firewall turned on, but if you suspect that it isn't, it is easy to turn the Firewall on.

1 Click the **Start** button, and click **Control Panel**. In the window that appears, type '**firewall**' into the search box. Click **Windows Firewall** in the results list. Click **Turn Windows Firewall on or off** in the left panel. You may have to enter your administrator password at this point.

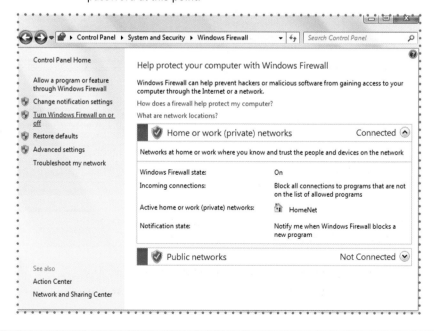

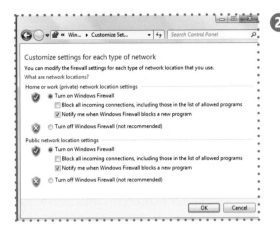

2 Under each of the network locations – such as Home or Work – click **Turn on Windows Firewall** for all the locations that you want to protect.

BE CAREFUL

Once turned on, you should never turn off Windows Firewall unless you are using another firewall program. Doing so will put your computer at risk from hackers and malware.

How can I get my firewall settings back to normal?

There are lots of settings in the Windows Firewall and you may feel that you've accidently changed a setting incorrectly. Don't worry. You can restore the Windows Firewall settings back to their original state.

1 Click the **Start** button, and click **Control Panel**. In the window that appears, type '**firewall**' into the search box. Click **Windows Firewall** in the results list. Click **Restore defaults** in the left panel. You may have to enter your administrator password at this point.

2 Click **Restore defaults** in the message that appears, then click **Yes**.

My program won't work with my firewall

Most programs are stopped from communicating with the outside world by Windows Firewall, thus protecting your computer. But some programs only work properly when connected to the internet, and many PC problems are related to programs being stopped from working properly by Windows Firewall.

If you need to allow a program to communicate through your firewall, you need to tell Windows Firewall to allow it through.

BE CAREFUL

Make sure that you trust the program you are giving permission to communicate through the firewall. If you have any doubts, contact the software manufacturer for advice.

1 Click the **Start** button, and click **Control Panel**. In the window that appears, type '**firewall**' into the search box. Click **Windows Firewall** in the results list.

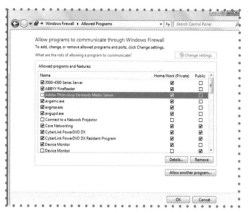

2 Click **Allow a program or feature through Windows Firewall** in the left panel, then click **Change settings**. You may have to enter your administrator password at this point.

3 Tick the box next to the program that you want to allow to communicate through the firewall, and choose the locations – such as Home – where permission is granted to the program. Click **OK** once done.

I can't play online games with others because of my firewall
Sometimes you might encounter a problem where your firewall will prevent activities, such as online gaming with others. To solve this, you need to open a port in your firewall using a firewall wizard.

1 Click the **Start** button, and click **Control Panel**. In the window that appears, type '**firewall**' into the search box. Click **Windows Firewall** in the results list. Click **Advanced settings** in the left panel. You may have to enter your administrator password at this point.

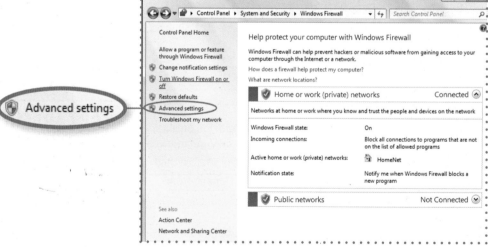

2 In the Windows Firewall with Advanced Settings window, click **Inbound Rules** in the left pane, followed by **New Rule** in the right pane. The New Inbound Rule Wizard will start. Follow the on-screen instructions.

CONNECTING DEVICES

By reading and following all the steps in this chapter, you will get to grips with:

▶ **How to identify and fix USB connection problems**

▶ **Tackling problems connecting digital cameras, hard drives or camcorders**

▶ **Solving problems connecting wireless Bluetooth devices, such as mice**

▶ Connecting devices

GENERAL USB PROBLEMS

There are many ways to connect devices, such as printers and digital cameras, to a computer. The most popular is the universal serial bus (USB) connector. This standard connection is designed to attach external devices, including hard drives and camcorders, to a computer and transfer data at high speeds between the device and the computer.

But sometimes plugging in a USB device doesn't work as expected – from the device not appearing at all to it not getting enough power from the USB port to power up.

The USB device isn't working at all
USB devices are designed to just plug straight into a computer and work, without needing any configuration. Try running the Hardware and Devices troubleshooter in Windows 7 to see if it can automatically fix the problem:

1 Click the **Start** button, then click **Control Panel**. In the Control Panel search box, type '**troubleshooter**' then click **Troubleshooting**.

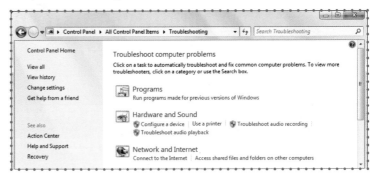

2 In the **Hardware and Sound** section, click **Configure a device**. You may have to enter your administrator password at this point.

3 Follow the instructions on screen to see if that solves the problem.

If the device is still refusing to work, you could have one of the following problems:

Windows can't find a USB driver for the device

Most times, Windows should automatically find and install the driver to communicate with the USB device, but if it can't find the correct USB driver, you'll need to take steps to install the right driver. See page 186 for advice on installing and updating drivers.

The device has a hardware problem or faulty driver

If it still isn't working, check whether the device – such as an MP3 player or digital camera – works when you plug it into another computer, if you have access to one. If it doesn't work, check the status of the USB device to see if it has a faulty driver:

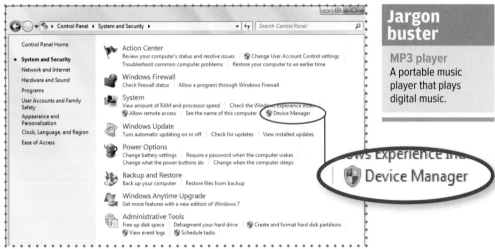

1 Click the **Start** button, then click **Control Panel**. In the Control Panel window, click **System and Security**, then click **Device Manager**. You may have to enter your administrator password at this point.

2 Double-click the relevant device category, such as Disk drives, then see if there is an entry for the device that is proving a problem.

139

Jargon buster

Port
A computer socket into which you plug equipment.

3 Right-click the entry for the USB device, and click **Properties**. In the **General** tab, look in the **Device status** box to see if it lists the problem. If you think the driver is faulty, then contact the USB device manufacturer to get a replacement.

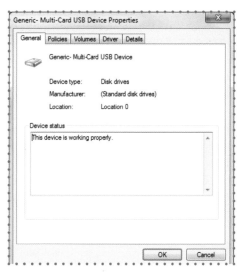

The USB port is broken

Try connecting the device to another USB port on your computer to see if the problem lies with one specific USB port. While rare, USB ports can become defective. If the device works with another USB port on your computer, use that and consider getting the defective USB port repaired.

Lack of power from the USB port

Some devices, such as portable hard drives, draw power from the USB port to run. Some USB ports do not supply enough power to run certain devices. Try inserting the USB device into another USB port on your computer, and unplugging all other USB devices to ensure it can draw the maximum amount of power from the USB port.

I get a 'Hi-speed USB device is plugged into a non-hi-speed USB hub' error message

Many high-speed USB devices that handle lots of data, such as a portable hard drive, need to be connected to a USB 2.0 port on your computer. Most computers today have USB 2.0 ports as standard, but to check:

1 Click the **Start** button, then click **Control Panel**. In the Control Panel window, click **System and Security**, then click **Device Manager**. You may have to enter your administrator password at this point.

2 Double-click the **Universal Serial Bus** controllers, if the word 'Enhanced' appears alongside any of the listed controls, your computer has USB 2.0 installed.

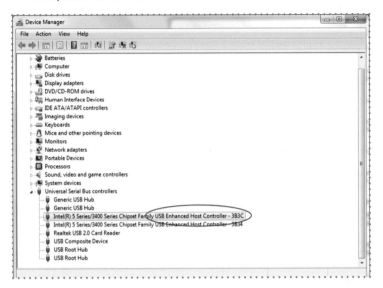

3 If your computer has USB 2.0 ports, the drivers needed for those ports to work properly on your computer may be missing. See page 186 for advice on installing and updating drivers.

⏵ Connecting devices

PRINTER CONNECTION PROBLEMS

A printer can experience connection problems for a number of reasons, with results varying from Windows 7 not recognizing it in the first place to it stopping working when you want to print a document.

If your printer is a USB model and connected to a USB port on your computer, you should check to see if the USB connection is at fault. See page 138 for advice on general USB problems and advice on how to solve them.

Try running the Hardware and Devices troubleshooter in Windows 7 to see if it can automatically fix the problem.

1 Click the **Start** button, then click **Control Panel**. In the Control Panel search box, type '**troubleshooter**' then click **Troubleshooting**.

2 In the **Hardware and Sound** section, click **Configure a device**. You may have to enter your administrator password at this point.

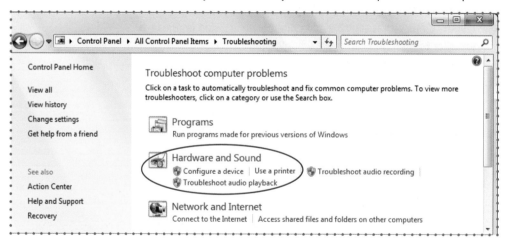

3 Follow the instructions on screen to see if that solves the problem.

Printer still not working?
Some printer-specific problems are listed below.

My printer often stops working when I'm printing a number of documents and I have to restart my computer.
Your printer software organizes jobs into a queue and, if one job fails, this can prevent any other work from being done. To access the print queue to find out what's happening:

1 Click the **Start** button, then click **Devices and printers** and double-click your printer. Look at the **Status** column. This should tell you if a job has failed and why.

2 To delete the job and get the queue moving again, click on the job and click **Cancel** from the top menu.

Printer connection problems
If you've connected a printer to your computer and it doesn't work – or mysteriously stops working – you might need to reinstall or update its driver. See page 186 for advice on updating and installing drivers.

Sharing your printer
There are several ways to network a printer. Some have Ethernet ports, so you can connect them directly to a network. However, most home printers use a USB or parallel connection, which means you can network them in one of two ways. You can buy a USB print server that allows wireless access to your printer from any computer on your network, but these can be quite expensive.

A cheaper option is to share your printer on the network via the PC it's attached to. The downside is that this PC has to be switched on whenever you want to print.

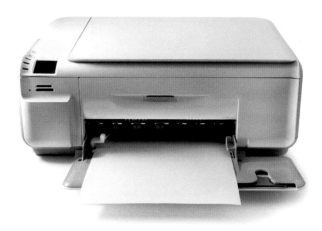

CAMERA CONNECTION PROBLEMS

If you've plugged your digital camera into your computer's USB port and it doesn't appear to be working at all, you could have one of the following problems:

▶ Make sure the cables are securely connected, and the camera is switched on.

▶ The camera may need to be set to a special mode to connect to a computer successfully – check the user manual to see if that is the case.

▶ Make sure that the hardware is working properly. Try running the Hardware and Devices troubleshooter in Windows 7 to see if it can automatically fix the problem with your camera's connection:

1 Click the **Start** button, then click **Control Panel**. In the Control Panel search box, type '**troubleshooter**' then click **Troubleshooting**.

2 In the **Hardware and Sound** section, click **Configure a device**. You may have to enter your administrator password at this point.

3 Follow the instructions on screen to see if that solves the problem.

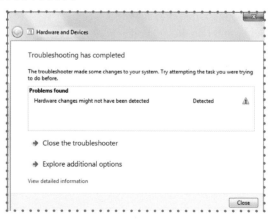

▶ Make sure that you have the correct driver for your camera so that Windows 7 can recognize it. See page 186 for advice on updating and installing drivers.

▶ If you have managed to connect your camera previously, the USB port on your computer may have stopped working. Try connecting it to another USB port, or see page 138 for advice on fixing general USB problems.

My camera connects to my computer, but Windows can't find any photos
There are several reasons why Windows may connect to your camera but has difficulties in finding the photos.

▶ Ensure that the memory card is in the camera.

▶ Ensure that you have not imported the photos before – Windows won't import photos that you have previously been imported.

▶ You may have accidently deleted the photos from the camera's memory card. If you suspect this is the case, see page 155 for advice on recovering accidently deleted photos.

▶ Double check that your camera doesn't store photos in several places, such as a memory card or an internal hard drive, and ensure that the camera settings allow those photos to be read from that location by Windows. Check the camera's user manual for information on how to do this.

Jargon buster

Memory card
A removable storage device, which holds images taken with a camera. They come in a variety of sizes and there are several types including Compact Flash, Multimedia and SD cards as well as Sony's Memory Stick format.

connecting devices

CAMCORDER CONNECTION PROBLEMS

Getting your computer to recognize your camcorder when you plug it in can sometimes be a problem. Often, the problem is specific to the camcorder or video software you are using, and you should check the help section of the manufacturer's website. But some general connection problems can be quickly fixed.

My computer isn't recognizing my camcorder using USB

First, check the basics, ensuring that the camcorder is both switched on and plugged into the mains using its own power supply. Some connection problems are due to running the camcorder only from its battery pack. It's also worth swapping the cable you are using to connect the camcorder in case there is a problem with the cable.

Make sure that the hardware is working properly. Try running the Hardware and Devices troubleshooter in Windows 7 to see if it can automatically fix the problem with your camcorder's connection:

1 Click the **Start** button, then click Control Panel. In the **Control Panel** search box, type '**troubleshooter**' then click **Troubleshooting**.

2 In the **Hardware and Sound** section, click **Configure a device**. You may have to enter your administrator password at this point.

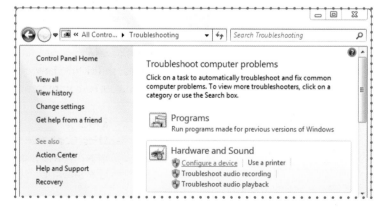

3 Follow the instructions on screen to see if that solves the problem.

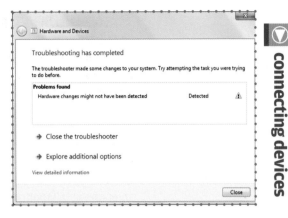

Make sure that you have the correct driver for your camera so that Windows 7 can recognize it. See page 186 for advice on updating and installing drivers.

If you have managed to connect your camera previously, the USB port on your computer may have stopped working. Try connecting it to another USB port, or see page 138 for advice on fixing general USB problems.

My computer isn't recognizing my camcorder using IEEE 1394 (FireWire)
Some camcorders use a special connection called IEEE 1394. You may need to manually update the IEEE 1394 driver for Windows 7.

1 Click the **Start** button, then type '**devmgmt.msc**' into the search box.

2 In the results panel, click the device tree and expand the **IEEE 1394 Bus host controllers** arrow in the right-hand panel.

3 Right-click the host controller note, then click **Update driver software** from the pop-up menu.

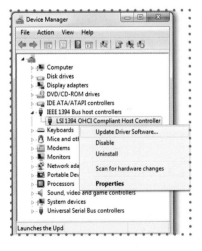

4 Click **Browse my computer for driver software**, then click **Let me pick from a list of device drivers on my computer**. Tick the **Show compatible hardware** box.

5 Click the **1394 OHCI Compliant Host Controller (Legacy)** option, then click **Next** to update the driver.

HARD DRIVE CONNECTION PROBLEMS

Most external hard drives connect via the USB port, and simply plug in and automatically appear in Windows ready to store your data. Sometimes, hard drives aren't seen by Windows – and that can be due to the USB connection or because the hard drive isn't formatted if it is new.

My computer isn't recognizing my external hard drive

Make sure that the external hard drive is both switched on and plugged into the mains using its own power supply if that is available. Some external hard drive problems are due to it being solely powered through the USB port, which might not be able to supply enough power to run it properly. It's also worth swapping the cable you are using to connect the hard drive in case there is a problem with the cable.

Make sure that the hardware is working properly. Try running the Hardware and Devices troubleshooter in Windows 7 to see if it can automatically fix the problem with your hard drive's connection:

1 Click the **Start** button, then click **Control Panel**. In the Control Panel search box, type '**troubleshooter**' then click **Troubleshooting**.

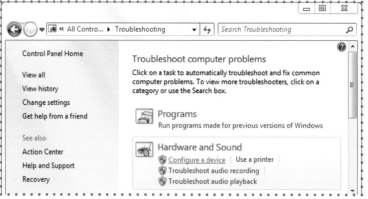

2 In the **Hardware and Sound** section, click **Configure a device**. You may have to enter your administrator password at this point.

3 Follow the instructions on screen to see if that solves the problem.

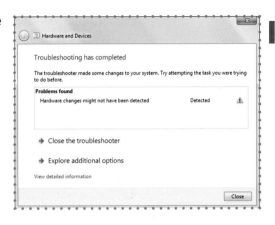

Make sure that you have the correct driver for your hard drive so that Windows 7 can recognize it. See page 186 for advice on updating and installing drivers.

If you have managed to connect your hard drive previously, the USB port on your computer may have stopped working. Try connecting it to another USB port, or see page 138 for advice on fixing general USB problems.

Connecting and formatting the hard drive

If the USB port and the cables are working fine, and the drive is drawing enough power, it may be that Windows can't see it because it needs to be initialized – made ready for use:

1 Click the **Start** button, then type '**Disk Management**' in the search box and press **Enter**.

If the hard drive appears in the list of detected drives, it may need initializing before Windows will recognise it outside of the Disk Management program.

2 Right-click the external hard drive in the **Disk Management** window, then click **Initialize Disk** (or **Format** if Initialize Disk isn't listed as an option).

3 In the Initialize Disk message box, select the hard drive to be initialized. Click **OK**.

It may take some time for a hard drive to be initialized. Do not unplug or turn off the power to the drive during this time.

BE CAREFUL

Initializing a hard drive will erase all data that is already stored on it. Only erase a hard drive if it is new, you have backed up any data on it, or you are sure you don't mind losing the data it contains.

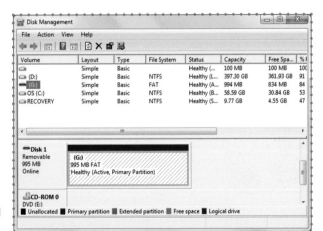

Connecting devices

BLUETOOTH CONNECTION PROBLEMS

Bluetooth is a popular, short-range wireless type of connection that many smaller devices use to communicate with a computer. Typical Bluetooth devices include wireless computer mice, PDAs, mobile phones and some MP3 players.

My Bluetooth device isn't seen by my computer
The first port of call is to remove and then reinstall the Bluetooth device that is causing problems:

❶ Click the **Start** button, then click **Control Panel**. In the Control Panel window, click **Hardware and Sound**, then click **Bluetooth Devices**.

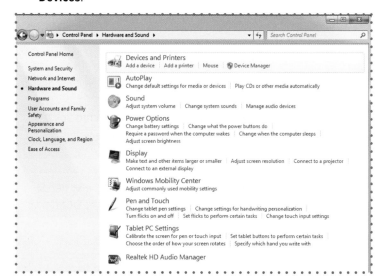

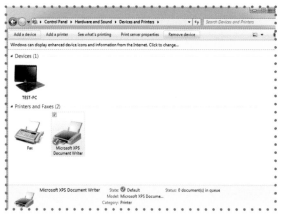

❷ In the list of devices, select the device that isn't working – such as Wireless Mouse – and click **Remove**.

3 Click **Add**, then on the Bluetooth device press the reset button or make it discoverable according to the device's user manual.

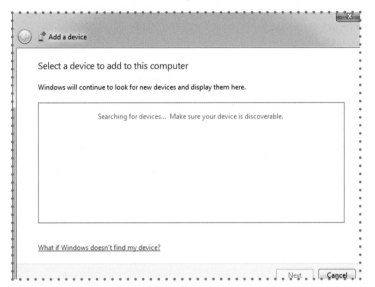

TRY THIS

Make sure the Bluetooth device is turned on and that the batteries don't need to be replaced – a common problem that means it won't connect successfully to your PC.

4 Tick the **My device is set up and ready to be found** tick box, then click **Next**. Repeat the last two steps if the device is not found. When the device is found, click **Next**.

5 Follow the rest of the steps that appear on screen. The device should now automatically reconnect each time you place it near your computer.

I need to reinstall my Bluetooth device

Ensure that your device's Bluetooth adapter is connected to your computer and turned on or, if your computer has a built-in Bluetooth adapter, that it is switched on. Ensure that your device is turned on and discoverable.

To reinstall a Bluetooth printer

Click the **Start** button, then click **Control Panel**. In the Control Panel window, click **Hardware and Sound**, then click **Printers**, then click **Add a printer**.

To reinstall a Bluetooth mobile phone

Click the **Start** button, then click **Control Panel**. In the Control Panel window, click **Hardware and Sound**, then click **Bluetooth Devices**, then click **Add**.

To reinstall a Bluetooth keyboard or mouse

Click the **Start** button, then click **Control Panel**. In the Control Panel window, click **Hardware and Sound**, then click **Bluetooth Devices**, then click **Add**.

My Bluetooth device still won't connect to my computer

Bluetooth is a short-range communications technology – so make sure that you haven't positioned the Bluetooth device too far from your computer.

Check your Bluetooth device isn't placed near other items that emit radio frequencies, such as microwaves, cordless phones and home wireless routers.

Check that other Bluetooth devices are not trying to connect to your Bluetooth device, such as a Bluetooth camera attempting to connect to a Bluetooth printer. Turn off all other Bluetooth devices and try connecting the main Bluetooth device to your computer following the previous steps.

Ensure that the right Bluetooth device is being discovered by your computer. You may have several Bluetooth devices of a similar nature in range, such as two mobile phones, that can cause connection confusion.

Ensure that your computer allows Bluetooth devices to connect:

1 Click the **Start** button, then click **Control Panel**. In the Control Panel window, click **Hardware and Sound,** then click **Bluetooth Devices**.

2 Click the **Options** tab, then tick the **Allow Bluetooth devices to connect to this computer** tick box, then click **OK**.

PHOTOS, MUSIC & VIDEO

By reading and following all the steps in this chapter, you will get to grips with:

 How to troubleshoot importing, editing and sharing photos

 How to fix audio and music download and playback problems

 How to stop video problems and share your home video

PROBLEMS WITH PHOTOS

There are lots of ways to import, view and edit photos in Windows 7 – and there are lots of different photo editing programs, each with their own ways of working.

Microsoft has a free photo program for Windows 7 called Windows Live Photo Gallery that can import, arrange, edit and share photos. You can download Windows Live Photo Gallery for free from http://download. live.com/photogallery. The help and advice in this book deals with Windows Live Photo Gallery – see the manufacturer's website of your particular photo-editing program if it is different for help and advice.

I can't import photos from my digital camera
Importing photos is usually straightforward, but you may have a problem with your camera's connection. See page 144 for help with camera connections. To import photos from a camera:

1 Connect the camera to your computer's USB port and switch the camera on.

2 In the **AutoPlay** box that appears, click **Import pictures and videos using Windows**. Click **Import**, and a window will appear showing the imported photos.

The AutoPlay box isn't appearing so I can't import my photos
AutoPlay may be turned off on your computer, so it won't appear when you plug in your camera. But you can still import your photos:

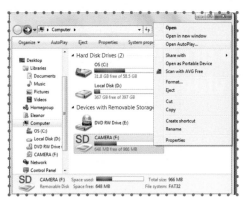

1 Click the **Start** button, then click **Computer**.

2 In the window in the left-hand navigation pane, right-click the icon of your digital camera, then click **Open AutoPlay...**. Click **Import pictures and videos using Windows,** and a window will appear showing the imported photos.

I can't choose which photos to import from my camera

To prevent duplicate photos being imported, Windows Live Photo Gallery will only import your newest photos. You can review and delete the photos that have been imported in Windows Live Photo Gallery once the import has happened.

I've imported my photos, but now I can't find them

When you import photos onto your computer – either from a digital camera or by another method such as from a memory card or scanner – they are by default placed in the Pictures folder. You can check that the import location is somewhere you expect in Windows Live Photo Gallery by following these steps:

1 Click the **Start** button, then **All Programs**, then click **Windows Live**, then **Windows Live Photo Gallery**. Once Windows Live Photo Gallery is open, click **File**, then click **Options**, and then click the **Import** tab.

2 Use the pop-up menu to set the import location for Cameras, ensuring it points to the **Pictures** folder.

3 Alternatively, click the **Restore defaults** button to return Windows Live Photo Gallery to its original settings.

Why do I have to enter a tag when I import my photos?

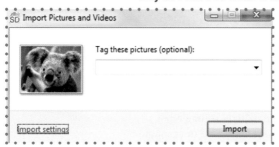

The short answer is: you don't. Tags are words that you attach to your picture when you import it to help describe it, such as 'family' or 'holiday'. You can then later use tags to quickly search and find specific types of photo. But the tag message can be annoying, so you can switch it off:

1 Connect the camera to your computer's USB port and switch the camera on.

2 In the **AutoPlay** box that appears, click **Import pictures and videos using Windows**. Click **Import settings** in the **Import Pictures and Video** box that appears. Untick **Prompt for a tag on import**, then click **OK**.

My photos are being automatically rotated when I import them

Some digital cameras are able to tell Windows whether a photo was taken in landscape or portrait, and Windows will attempt to automatically rotate the photo when it is imported. If you want to turn it off:

1 Click the **Start** button, then **All Programs**, then click **Windows Live**, then **Windows Live Photo Gallery**. Once Windows Live Photo Gallery is open, click **File**, then click **Options**, and then click the **Import** tab.

2 Untick the **Rotate pictures on import** tick box, then click **OK**.

I can't edit my photos in Windows Live Photo Gallery

It can be frustrating when you have successfully managed to import a photo and you find that you can't edit it. If you try to edit a photo and get a message that says the photo can't be changed, it could be for one of the following reasons:

The photo is read-only

What this means You won't be able to save any changes made to the photo.

What you can do Change the photo's attributes so that the photo is no longer read-only. To do this, open **Windows Live Photo Gallery**, then right-click the photo and choose **Properties**. Click the **Security** tab, then click the **Edit...** button to change the permissions for the photo. Choose a username (this is usually your account name) and make sure that **Allow** is ticked alongside **Full control**, **Modify**, **Read & execute**, **Read**, and **Write** settings.

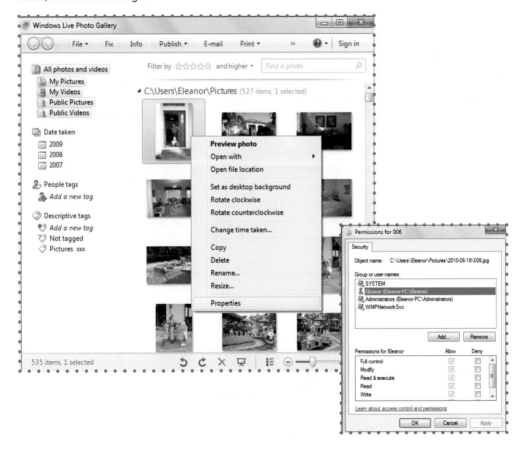

The photo is stored on read-only media
What this means Changes to photos saved on read-only media, such as a DVD, won't be able to be saved to the read-only media.
What you can do Copy your photos from the read-only media to your computer. See page 61 for help with moving files.

Windows doesn't understand what type of file the photo is
What this means The photo may be saved in a format that Windows Live Photo Gallery doesn't recognize, such as a special file used by your digital camera. Some files, such as RAW and GIF are not supported by Windows Live Photo Gallery.
What you can do Check the instructions that came with your camera to ensure you are saving photos in a format that Windows Live Photo Gallery understands, such as JPG or TIF.

The photo may have been moved or deleted while it was open
What this means The photo file may have been moved or deleted from your hard drive while it was also open in Windows Live Photo Gallery. It will continue to appear in Windows Live Photo Gallery even though the file has been moved or deleted, and Windows Live Photo Gallery won't be able to save your edited changes.
What you can do Check that the file hasn't been moved to another location or placed in the Recycle Bin. Restore the file to its original location.

The photo format doesn't work with tags
What this means The photo file may be of a type that doesn't support tags added in Windows Live Photo Gallery.
What you can do You can still add tags, but they won't be visible to Windows in the file Explorer or on another computer. Resave the file as a tag-compatible type, such as JPG or TIF.

Windows can't find the original file because it is stored on a networked device
What this means If you opened the file over a network, for example the file is stored on a networked hard drive or another computer on the network, that device may no longer be available on the network. This has the same effect of moving or deleting the file, and Windows Live Photo Gallery can't find the original file to save your edited changes to.
What you can do Check that the networked device or computer is working and connected to the network. See page 76 for help and advice on networking.

Help! I've edited a picture and I want to go back to the original version

If you've made changes to a photo, but aren't satisfied with the changes you made using the Fix pane in Windows Live Photo Gallery, you can go back to the original version. Windows Live Photo Gallery always saves a copy of the original photo when you work on it using the Fix pane. To restore it:

1 In Windows Live Photo Gallery in the **Fix** pane, click **Revert**.

2 Click **Revert to original**.

PROBLEMS WITH MUSIC

Music and audio playback and listening problems can be a real pain – from sound not coming from your computer to problems playing back and storing audio files on your PC.

Help! My computer isn't playing back any audio

If you hit Play and your computer isn't making any noise, it could be either a hardware problem, such as a problem with your speakers or sound card driver, or a software problem, such as Windows Media Player not working correctly.

First, rule out physical audio problems, such as sound card issues. Full advice on dealing with this kind of sound problem is detailed on page 20.

Try using the Windows Media Player Settings troubleshooter

If you are still having audio problems and have ruled out the solutions

on page 20, then try running the Windows Media Player Settings troubleshooter. This will examine the settings for Windows Media Player – the default program used to play music and video on your computer – to ensure that any music you've ripped from a CD or downloaded from the web can be played successfully.

1 Click the **Start** button, then click **Control Panel**. In the Control Panel search box, type '**troubleshooter**', and then click **Troubleshooting**.

2 Click **View all** in the results list, then click **Windows Media Player Settings**. Follow the on-screen instructions for fixing any problems that the troubleshooter identifies.

Help! I have problem copying music onto my computer

Copying a CD onto a computer transfers the songs into a format, such as MP3, that Windows and Windows Media Player understand, and stores them in a dedicated space in Windows. You can then synchronize your devices, such as an MP3 player, with these files so you can take your music with you wherever you go.

I can't find the music files that I've just copied onto my computer

When you copy music files from a CD onto your computer, or you download music files from an online store such as Amazon.com, the music files are placed in the Music library. To change the default location:

1 Click the **Start** button, then click **All Programs**, then click **Windows Media Player**. Click **Organize**, then **Options**, then click the **Rip Music** tab. Click the **Change...** button to choose the location where music is stored on your computer.

The file names for my music files are strange

If you are unhappy with the automatic naming given to music files that are downloaded or copied to your computer, you can change them using Windows Media Player:

1 Click the **Start** button, then click **All Programs**, then click **Windows Media Player**. Click **Organize**, then **Options**, then click the **Rip Music** tab. **Click the File Name...** button, then tick the options, such as Artist, that you'd like in the file name. Click **OK**.

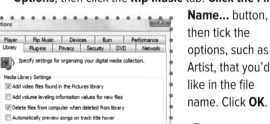

2 Click the **Library** tab, then tick **Rename music files using rip music settings**. Click **OK**.

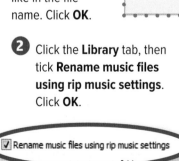

✓ Rename music files using rip music settings

▶ Photos, music & video

The audio I copy has skipping and popping problems
While it is possible to listen to other music files while you are copying music to your computer without problems, performing other tasks such as using other programs can mean that the copied music doesn't fully copy intact. To get the best copy, avoid performing other activities with your computer while Windows Media Player copies music to your computer.

Windows Media Player problems and tips
As Windows Media Player is the default audio and video player in Windows 7, many problems with audio playback can be fixed within Windows Media Player. Here are some common issues and solutions:

How can I listen to internet radio on my computer?
You don't need to download a special program on your computer to listen to radio stations on the internet. Windows Media Player has its own radio service that is hidden away:

1 Click the **Start** button, then click **All Programs**, then click **Windows Media Player**. With Windows Media Player open, click the **Media Guide** tab, then click the **Internet Radio** link. A list of online radio stations will appear.

2 Click on different genres to narrow your selection, or click the **Search** link to enter in a search term, such as 'jazz'. Click a station name to play.

My internet radio station is playing sound intermittently
If you are listening to online music, such as an internet radio station, and it regularly cuts out for periods of time, you need to increase the buffer – a space that fills up with music before it starts playing, ensuring that there is always enough audio downloaded from the internet to give smooth playback:

1 Click the **Start** button, then click **All Programs**, then click **Windows Media Player.** With Windows Media Player open, click **Organize**, then click **Options**.

2 Click the **Performance** tab, and increase the Buffer value to a value such as 30 seconds of content. This will download 30 seconds of music before playback begins, always ensuring that you have enough music downloaded for smooth playback.

photos, music & video

My audio files don't open in Windows Media Player

Some files that can be played in Windows Media Player may have been set up so that they try to open another program instead, such as a recently installed sound-editing program. To set-up Windows Media Player to play the files you want:

1 Click the **Start** button, then click **Computer**, then locate a file type you want to play in Windows Media Player. Right-click the file, and choose **Open with...**, then click **Choose default program**.

2 Click the program, such as Windows Media Player, that you want to open the file. Tick the **Always use the selected program to open this kind of file** tick box, then click **OK**.

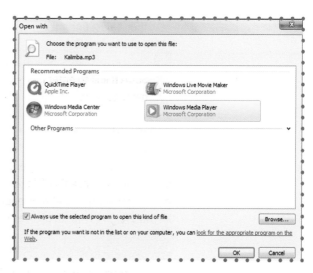

The volume differences between songs is really irritating

It can be irritating to have to reach for the volume control for each new song that plays because each song has been recorded at a different volume level. This can happen if you listen to songs from various different albums. You can reduce the sharp volume changes between songs that were encoded in Windows Media Audio (WMA) or MP3 formats by Windows Media Player by using volume levelling:

1 Click the **Start** button, then click **All Programs**, then click **Windows Media Player**. With Windows Media Player open switch to **Now Playing** mode.

2 Right-click an open space in the Player in Now Playing mode, then select **Enhancements**, then click **Crossfading and auto volume leveling**.

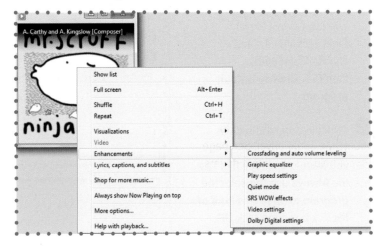

3 Click the **Turn on Auto Volume Leveling** link. To add volume-levelling to a file, you need to play the entire file (such as an audio file) with auto-leveling turned on. Click the **Close** button in the **Crossfading and auto volume leveling** box when done.

Music skips and breaks up when I play it back on my computer

If you are using Windows Media Player to listen to audio, and the end of the songs begins to break up and stutter or skip, your computer's speaker enhancements could be the culprit. You should disable all speaker enhancements and, if that solves the problem, update your audio drivers:

1 Click the **Start** button, then click **Control Panel**. In the Control Panel search box, type '**sound**', then click **Sound** on the results. Click the **Playback** tab, then click **Speakers**, then click **Properties**.

2 Click the **Enhancements** tab, then tick the **Disable all sound effects** tick box.

If this resolves your audio playing problem, then you will need to update the audio driver. See page 186 for help with updating drivers.

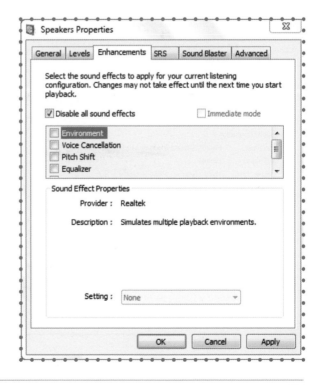

VIDEO PLAYBACK PROBLEMS

With computers becoming ever more powerful, and Windows 7 including plenty of video features, it's not surprising that computers can be used both to watch video and also to edit and share video. Video playback problems include not being able to watch video at all or being plagued with choppy video or DVDs that don't work properly.

Help! I can't see any video on my computer

If you hit Play in your video program, such as Windows Media Player and your computer doesn't play video back, it could be either a hardware problem – such as a problem with the graphics card that displays an image on the screen – or a software problem, such as Windows Media Player not working correctly.

Solving graphics card problems

The graphics card is a device that is responsible for sending the image from your computer to the screen. Many different manufacturers will provide free updates to graphics cards that can solve video-display and playback problems. To find out what graphics card your computer has:

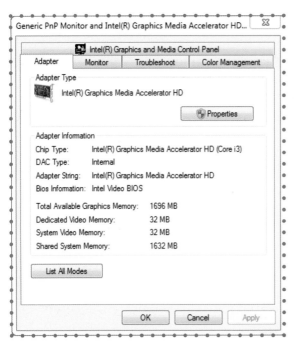

1 Click the **Start** button, then click **Control Panel**. In the Control Panel, click **Adjust screen resolution** located under **Appearance and Personalization**.

2 Click **Advanced settings**, then click the **Adapter** tab. Here you can see details of your graphics card.

3 Visit the support section of the website of the manufacturer of the graphics card for help and advice.

You may need to update the driver for your graphics card – this will bring it up to date. See page 186 for help on updating and installing new drivers.

Try using the Windows Media Player Settings troubleshooter

If you are still having video problems and have ruled out the graphics card, then try running the Windows Media Player Settings troubleshooter (see page 160). This will examine the settings for Windows Media Player – the default program used to play video on your computer – to ensure that any video can be played successfully.

I'm watching a DVD on my computer but I have sound problems

If you hit Play on your DVD and your DVD plays video, but doesn't have any sound or has choppy, broken sound it could be either a hardware problem – such as a problem with your speakers or sound card driver – or an incorrect setting in Windows.

First, rule out physical audio problems, such as sound card issues. Full advice on dealing with this kind of sound problem is detailed on page 20.

1 Click the **Speakers** button in the notification area of the taskbar. Move the sliders up to increase the speaker volume. Ensure the **Mute** button is not depressed.

To check the sound volume in Windows Media Player:

2 Click the **Start** button, then choose **All Programs**, then click **Windows Media Player**. Move the volume slider to adjust the volume. Ensure the **Mute** button isn't selected.

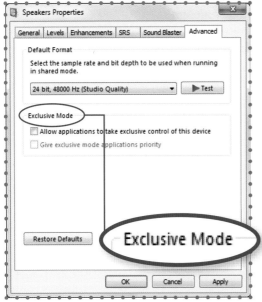

If the previous actions did not fix the problem with sound while watching a DVD in Windows 7, then you might need to adjust your audio settings:

1 Click the **Start** button, then click **Control Panel**. In Control Panel, click **Hardware and Sound**, then click **Sound**. Right-click the default playback device that has a green tick next to it, then click **Properties**.

2 Click the **Advanced** tab, then clear all settings in the **Exclusive Mode** box, then click **OK**.

The video in Windows 7 is really poor quality

Playing video back on a computer can use lots of the computer's resources, so you need to optimize the way that your computer is set up to play video as much as possible.

1 Click the **Start** button, then type '**Power options**' in the search box. Click the **Power Options** link in the results that appear, then click **Change plan settings** for the currently selected plan.

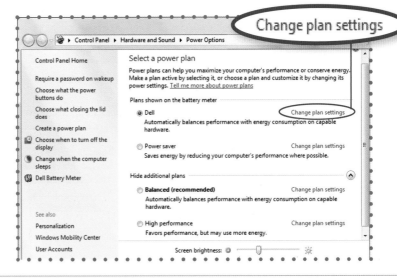

2 Click **Change advanced power settings**, and click the small cross in a box to expand the Multimedia settings section. Ensure that the **When playing video** setting is set to **Optimize video quality**.

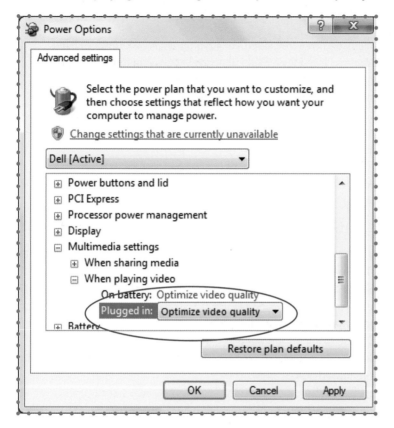

I get an error message that Windows Media Player cannot play the video file

You'll get this error message when Windows Media Player does not recognize the file format the video file is in, and so is unable to play it back. Windows Media Player uses codecs – small language programs that help it understand different types of video file – to play video. To see if a codec is available that can be downloaded and installed in Windows Media Player:

1 In the error message, click **Web Help**. This will take you to Microsoft's support site that can help you download the necessary codec.

VIDEO EDITING PROBLEMS

There are lots of ways to import, view and edit videos and home movies in Windows 7 – and there are lots of different video-editing programs, each with their own ways of working.

Microsoft has a free video-editing program for Windows 7 called Windows Live Movie Maker that can import, arrange, edit and share video. You can download Windows Live Movie Maker for free from http://download.live.com/moviemaker. The help and advice in this book deals with Windows Live Movie Maker – see the manufacturer's website of your particular video-editing program if it is different for help and advice.

Which format do I use to import video in Windows Live Movie Maker?
When you connect your camcorder to your computer, you can import video onto your computer in a particular type of file format. Unfortunately, there are lots of different file formats for video and if you choose the wrong one it can lead to problems playing back video. Here is a guide to problem-free video formats.

I'm importing from a camcorder
Choose to import the video as either Windows Media Video (WMV) or use the file format that the camera stores video in, such as Audio Video Interleaved (AVI).

I eventually want to play my video back on videotape
If you plan to save your video to video tape after editing it on your computer (rather than, say, DVD) then make sure you choose Audio Video Interleaved (AVI) as the video format you import your video on.

I have limited hard disk space on my computer
Different video formats take up different amounts of storage space on a computer, and that can mean if you choose the wrong format you could run out of space to import video from your camcorder. For example, importing an hour of video in the Windows Media Video (WMV) format will take around 1 GB of hard disk space. The same length of video will take around 13 GB of space if you import it in Audio Video Interlaced (AVI) format.

My computer is not very powerful

If you don't have a very fast computer with lots of memory, then it's worth importing video in Windows Media Video (WMV) format as this will use less computer resources and result in fewer dropped frames or video import problems.

I want to import my video as one long file, but it keeps saving as lots of different files

It can be an advantage to import your video clips as individual files when using Windows Live Movie Maker by importing video in the Windows Media Video format. But sometimes you might want to have all the video on your camcorder imported as one, single long file by importing as an Audio Video Interlaced file, for example. If you are doing this and the video keeps being saved into several files, it could be due to one of the following:

The video aspect ratio changed If you started recording video in one aspect ratio, such as standard (known as 4:3 ratio), and then used your camcorder to record a scene in widescreen (known as 16:9 ratio), Windows Live Movie Maker will save each segment of video with its own aspect ratio as a separate file.

The video format changes on the tape If your camcorder can record video in different formats, and you switch format mid-tape or video, Windows Live Movie Maker will save each video format as a separate file.

The DVD I recorded to in Windows won't play in my home DVD player

Recordable DVDs come in DVD-R and DVD+R (record once) formats, and DVD-RW, DVD+RW and DVD-RAM (rewriteable) formats. Older DVD players won't play all recordable DVD formats. Some that claim that they do only work consistently with a particular standard. Check your manual for details, then buy and use the appropriate discs.

It's also important to check that your disc has been formatted and finalized correctly for playback in a home DVD player. This should happen automatically when you use Windows Live Movie Maker.

I can't seem to share my video

Windows Live Movie Maker can share videos that you create directly on the website YouTube, but you will need to already have a YouTube account. To share a video:

1 Click the **Start** button, then click **All Programs**, then click **Windows Live Movie Maker**.

2 Open the video you want to share using the **File** menu, then click the **Home** tab and, in the **Sharing** section, click **Publish on YouTube**.

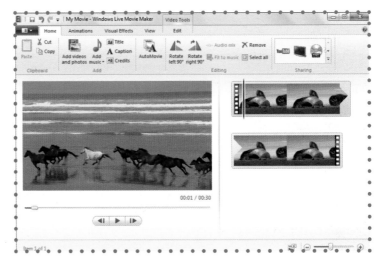

3 Enter your YouTube account name and password, then click **Sign In**. Give the video a title, search tags and select a category (such as Music) to publish the video on YouTube.

4 Select to make your movie public (anyone can see it) or private (only selected people can see it), then click **Publish**.

KEEP YOUR PC HEALTHY

By reading and following all the steps in this chapter, you will get to grips with:

- **How to keep files safely backed up and restore your PC if it goes wrong**

- **How to fix hard drive errors and update and install Windows drivers**

- **Speeding up your PC, keeping your PC clean, plus housekeeping tips**

Keep your PC healthy

BACKING UP FILES

Like any insurance, backing up can feel like a waste of time and money – until you really need it. Imagine how you'd feel if one day all your precious family photographs, videos of special events or your music collection just disappeared?

However, if you have a good backup strategy in place, there's no need to panic – you'll have a copy of your files and folders saved to a separate drive or perhaps online. From here, you can retrieve your files easily.

You can use a portable external hard drive or save to discs and store your data away from your home. Most external hard drives will come bundled with software, but this isn't as flexible as some stand-alone versions that you can buy separately.

External hard drives
External hard drives add storage space to a computer that's groaning under the weight of large software and music files. Plus, they're a great place to keep copies of all your important data should your hard drive break.

Desktop/stand-alone drives
Desktop drives sit next to your PC, connected most of the time. They come with an external power supply that needs its own mains plug. Most connect via USB. Choose a desktop drive if you want to add extra storage space to your PC for carrying out backups.

Portable drives
Portable hard drives are tiny. They don't need a separate external power supply, but instead draw the power from the PC via the USB cable. They tend to have less storage space than desktop drives, but their small size means they are more portable.

Network drives
If you have a home network, you could consider a network hard disk, which you can connect to your network so everyone can save their files onto it. The speed of a drive on your network will be directly affected by the slowest part of the network – for example your Wi-Fi connection or your router.

Backup software

Windows 7 includes backup software as part of the operating system. See page 176 for help on using it. You can also use commercial backup software programs.

There's no such thing as a one-size-fits-all backup solution. You don't necessarily need to back up everything on your computer. You really only need to make copies of everything that's important to you.

Good backup software will copy your files in a systematic, hassle-free way, making sure you have a copy of the latest version of your files. It will regularly back up everything to your external hard drive and even save a copy of your hard disk.

It's a good idea to back up once a week or more, depending on how vital your data is. A lot of programs will do it automatically for you at a preset time. Check whether the one you choose has this option.

Jargon buster

Wi-Fi
A wireless, high-speed networking system that can transfer data at high speeds across lots of different devices.

Keep your PC healthy

HOW TO BACK UP FILES

Windows 7 includes a Backup and Restore feature that can be used to create digital copies of your personal files and folders. It can be used to back up specific folders or everything in case of a crash. You will need to have a backup drive attached to the computer to back up your information – see page 174 for advice on choosing the right one:

1 Click the **Start** button, then click **Control Panel**. In the Control Panel, click **System and Security**, then click **Backup and Restore**.

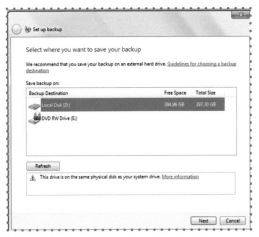

2 Click **Set up backup**, then follow the steps in the on-screen backup wizard. You may need to enter your administrator password at this point.

Windows will then create a backup according to the settings you made during the setup. You may have to wait a while for all the data to be backed up onto your backup storage drive.

You should set up a regular, scheduled backup when setting up the Backup and Restore wizard. Windows will then backup any new data you have added or changes to files onto the external storage at regular intervals.

To create an instant backup

If you have set up Backup and Restore and it is running according to a schedule, it is possible to override the schedule and perform an instant backup.

1 Click the **Start** button, then click **Control Panel**. In the Control Panel, click **System and Security**, then click **Backup and Restore**.

2 Click **Back up now**. You may need to enter your administrator password at this point.

How do I restore my backed up files?

If your files have been deleted, changed accidently or you need to restore the files you have previously backed up, follow these steps:

1 Click the **Start** button, then click **Control Panel**. In the Control Panel, click **System and Security**, then click **Backup and Restore**.

2 Click **Restore my files**.

3 If you want to restore just a few, specific files, click **Browse for files** or **Browse for folders**. Choose the ones to back up.

TRY THIS

You can search for backed up files in the **Backup and Restore** panel. Click **Search**, then type all or part of a file name, then click **Search**.

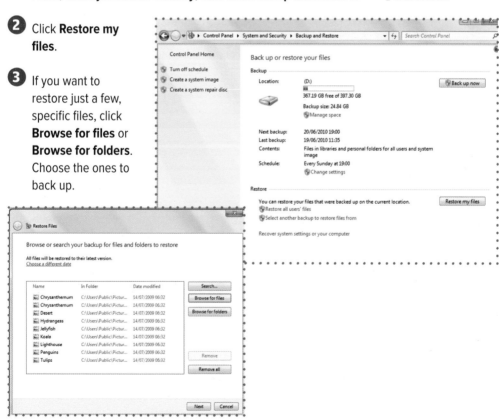

177

CREATING A SYSTEM REPAIR DISC

If something goes seriously wrong with your computer, it is important to have created a System Repair Disc. This can help you fix Windows 7 if a major error occurs, and is used if you don't have access to a Windows 7 installation disc or the recovery options – such as a recovery CD – that was supplied with your computer.

A System Repair Disc can be created at any time, and is a good idea to make one to help keep your computer healthy. You will need a blank CD or DVD to create one.

Creating a System Repair Disc

1 Click the **Start** button, then click **Control Panel**.

2 Click **System and Security**, then click **Backup and Restore**.

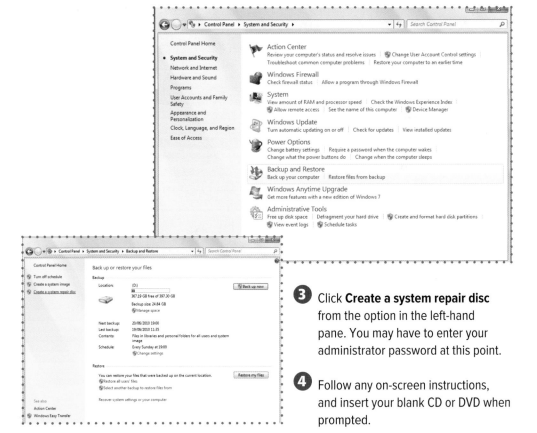

3 Click **Create a system repair disc** from the option in the left-hand pane. You may have to enter your administrator password at this point.

4 Follow any on-screen instructions, and insert your blank CD or DVD when prompted.

Using the System Repair Disc

If you're faced with a major problem, such as a serious problem with Windows, then the System Repair Disc can be used.

1 Place the system repair disk into your CD or DVD drive.

2 Restart your computer by pressing your computer's power button.

3 If Window's prompts you, press any key to start the computer from the System Repair Disc.

4 Confirm or change any **Language settings**, then click **Next**.

5 Select the **Startup Repair** option, and then click **Next**.

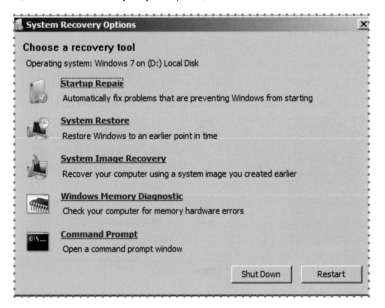

TRY THIS

If Windows asks you to install a Windows installation disc, it means that your computer doesn't have the files needed on its hard drive to create a System Repair Disc. You'll need to insert your Windows 7 installation disc to continue.

RESTORE YOUR COMPUTER

If your computer experiences a bad crash or major software problem, wouldn't it be great to wind back the clock to just before the crash when everything was working fine?

System Restore in Windows 7 does just that. It returns your computer's system files and programs to a time when everything was working properly, and you can see which files will be removed or added when your computer is restored.

System Restore uses 'restore points' that act like milestones for your PC. They can be created to a schedule or before a major task, such as installing software. If you need to, you can then use System Restore to return your PC to how it was when it saved a 'restore point'.

Setting up System Restore

Before you start using **System Restore**, it is important that you have closed all running programs and saved all open files. Once a restore point is set, your computer will also automatically restart itself, so only start this process when you are ready:

TRY THIS

If Windows asks you to install a Windows installation disc, it means that your computer doesn't have the files needed on its hard drive to create a System Repair Disc. You'll need to insert your Windows 7 installation disc to continue.

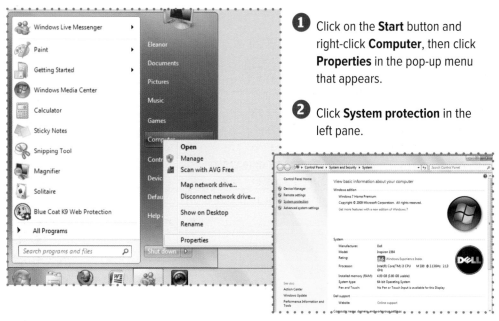

1 Click on the **Start** button and right-click **Computer**, then click **Properties** in the pop-up menu that appears.

2 Click **System protection** in the left pane.

3 Click on the **System Protection** tab, and then click **Create**.

4 Enter a description such as 'Restore point May 19, 2010' in the System Protection dialog box, then click **Create**.

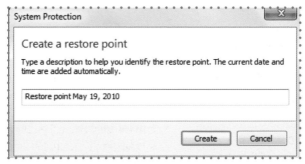

A restore point will now be automatically created and your computer will then restart. Once restarted, you can use your computer as normal and, if you encounter a problem, you can return your computer to the state it was in when you created the restore point.

Choosing a restore point to return your computer to

If you notice something going wrong with your computer, and you want to use a system restore point, how do you know the right one to pick? Typically, System Restore will recommend the most recently created restore point, but you can also select one based on it being before the time and date that you first noticed a problem. It also makes sense to make good use of the restore point description as detailed in Step 4 previously, so you can label the restore with information before you do something significant to your PC.

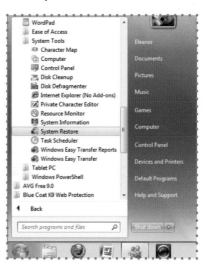

Using System Restore to recover your computer

If you do need to return the state of your computer to that of a previous restore point, follow these steps:

1 Click on the **Start** button, then choose **All programs** and navigate to **Accessories**, then **System Tools** in the menu.

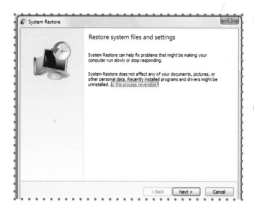

2 Click on **System Restore**, then click **Next** in the Restore system files and settings window. You may have to enter your administrator password at this point.

3 From the menu that appears, choose the restore point you'd like to return your computer to, such as the state it was in when you created the restore point 'Restore point May 19, 2010'.

4 Click **Next**, then click **Finish** on the **Confirm your restore point** window to begin restoring your computer.

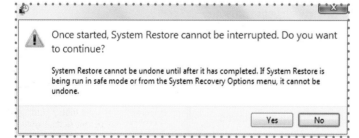

5 Click **Yes** on the **Once started, System Restore cannot be interrupted. Do you want to continue?** message.

It may take several minutes, but Windows 7 will be restored to the state it was in at the restore point you selected in Step 3. Once done, your computer will shut down and restart.

Can I reverse the changes System Restore makes?

If you accidently use a restore point that you didn't mean to, don't worry. System Restore automatically creates a second restore point so you can rewind your computer back to the point just before you used a restore point by mistake. To undo a restore point:

1 Click on the **Start** button, then choose **All programs** and navigate to **Accessories**, then **System Tools** in the menu.

2 Click on **System Restore**. You may have to enter your administrator password at this point.

3 Click **Undo System Restore**, and then click **Next**. If you're happy with your decision, click **Finish** and the restore point you accidentally created will be erased.

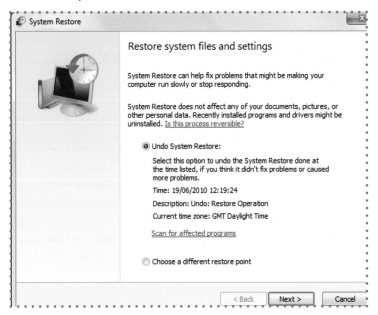

TRY THIS

System Restore only affects Windows 7 files such as system files, programs and other settings. It does not affect your personal data such as email, photos and documents.

TRY THIS

If you can't see your restore point, tick the **Show more restore points** tick box to see more than just the most recent restore points.

Storing System restore points

System restore points don't have a sell-by date, and are saved until the space allocated on your hard drive for keeping restore points is used up. If it runs out of space, the newest restore points will automatically overwrite the oldest restore points.

UPDATING WINDOWS AND PROGRAMS

Keeping your computer up to date is an important housekeeping task that can help fix glitches and niggles, as well as ensure that you are protected from faults and problems as they are discovered. Windows 7 has an automatic updating facility that will ensure that Windows updates are downloaded and installed as they become available. It is recommended that you use the automatic update feature in Windows.

Automatically download updates

1 Click the **Start** button, then type '**Update**' in the search box and then click **Windows Update** in the results list that appears.

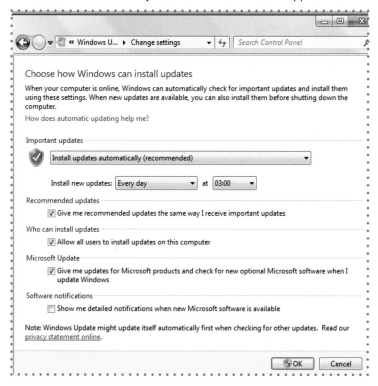

2 Click **Change settings** in the left pane, then under the **Important updates** section, choose the option you want, and under **Recommended updates** tick the **Give me recommended updates the same way I receive important updates** tick box. You may have to enter your administrator password at this point.

I'm having problems installing updates automatically

If you have set up automatic Windows updates, but you are having problems downloading them or installing them, you can use the Windows Update troubleshooter to fix common problems that can occur with Windows Update:

1 Click the **Start** button, then click **Control Panel**.

2 Type '**troubleshooter**' in the **Control Panel** search box, and click **Troubleshooting** in the list of results that appear.

3 In the Troubleshooting window, click **Fix problems with Windows Update** under the **System and Security** section.

4 Follow the on-screen instructions to check and automatically fix problems with Windows Update.

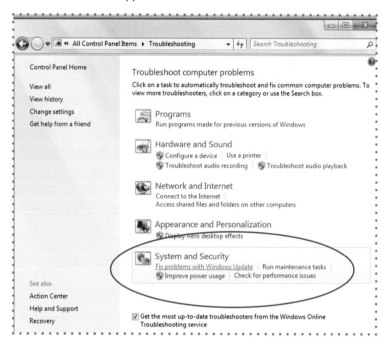

Windows Update keeps restarting my computer

This is normal once an update has been downloaded and installed. Once the installation is finished, Windows will show a message saying that it needs to restart to finish the update process.

If you do not want Windows to restart your computer straight away, click the **Postpone the restart** option. It's worth knowing that if you leave your computer unattended for a long period while Windows Update downloads and updates Windows, it will automatically restart the computer after a set time.

UPDATING AND INSTALLING DRIVERS

Many problems with hardware devices or your computer working properly can be traced back to problems with drivers. A driver is a small program that tells Windows and other software how to talk to a piece of hardware, such as how to print out a Word document on your printer.

If a hardware device isn't working properly, then you may need to update the driver. It's good practice to routinely update your drivers to help keep your PC healthy.

Options for updating drivers

▶ Windows Update can be set to automatically download and install recommended updates, including the latest drivers for your devices.
▶ You can often install a driver from any DVD or CD from the manufacturer that came with the hardware, such as a printer. This is handy for restoring the driver back to its 'factory settings'.
▶ You can download and update the driver yourself from the manufacturer's website. This is useful if Windows Update can't locate the driver for your device, and you can't locate a DVD or CD that includes the driver.

Using Windows Update to install drivers

Windows Update can be checked at any time to see if a new, updated driver has been made available for your device. It's useful to use Windows Update to locate an updated driver if you have just installed a new device, such as a printer:

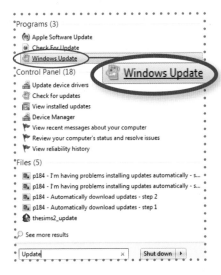

1 Ensure that you are connected to the internet.

2 Click on the **Start** button. In the search box, type '**Update**' and then click on **Windows Update** in the list of results.

3 Click **Check for updates** in the left pane.

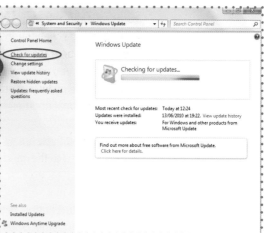

Windows Update will check online to see if any updates are available. Click the links to see more information about any available updates. You can also see if an update is listed as important, recommended or optional. Drivers will be included in all types of available update.

4 Click on the **Select the updates you want to install** page, and identify the updates relevant to your hardware devices.

5 Tick the box next to each driver that you want to install and update, and then click **OK**.

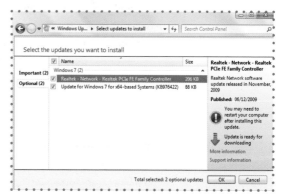

6 Click on the **Windows Update** page, and choose **Install updates**. You may have to enter your administrator password at this point. The drivers will then be installed on your computer.

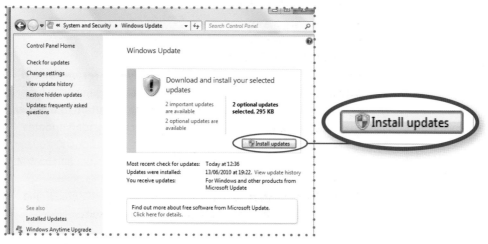

Automatically installing recommended updates to drivers

To keep your PC healthy, it's a good idea to set Windows Update to automatically check and download new driver updates, and to install them without you needing to do anything. Windows Update will only download and install important or recommended updates – you'll have to install optional updates manually following the steps above.

TRY THIS

You can let anyone who uses your computer install updates by ticking **Allow all users to install updates on this computer** in Windows Update.

1 Ensure that you are connected to the internet.

2 Using the mouse, click on the **Start** button. In the search box, type '**Update**' and then click on **Windows Update** in the list of results.

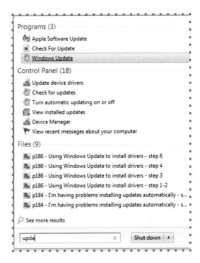

3 Click **Change settings** in the left pane.

4 Click on an item in the list under **Important updates** to determine which updates to automatically download and install.

5 Tick **Give me recommended updates the same way I receive important updates** in the **Recommended updates** section, then click **OK**. You may have to enter your administrator password at this point.

Manually downloading and installing drivers

While it's a good idea to let Windows Update take care of updating software and drivers automatically, sometimes you have to find a driver manually online:

1 Make sure you are connected to the internet, and using your web browser, go to the website of the manufacturer of your hardware device.

2 Search in the support section of the website to locate and download the driver you need.

3 Once located and downloaded, follow the installation instructions on the website. Most drivers will install themselves automatically when they are downloaded – you just need to double-click on the downloaded driver to start the installation process.

TRY THIS

If you are buying a new device, such as a printer, go to the Windows 7 Compatibility Center online (www. microsoft.com/windows/ compatibility/windows-7/en-us/default.aspx). It holds a list of devices that have been tested to work with Windows 7.

Manually installing drivers

If the driver doesn't automatically install in Step 3 (above), then you can install it manually. You will need to be logged in as an administrator to do this.

1 Click the **Start** button, then click **Control Panel**.

2 In the Control Panel, click **System and Security**, then in the System section, click **Device Manager**. You may have to enter your administrator password at this point.

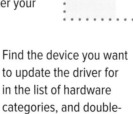

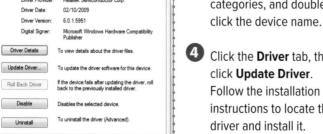

3 Find the device you want to update the driver for in the list of hardware categories, and double-click the device name.

4 Click the **Driver** tab, then click **Update Driver**. Follow the installation instructions to locate the driver and install it.

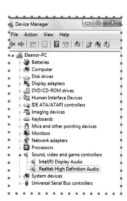

MY HARD DRIVE IS SLOW

When a large file is stored on a hard drive, Windows often stores parts of the file in various locations. This fragmentation of files means your computer hard drive has to work harder to open files and work, and it can slow down your PC. It's possible for all hard drives – including USB keys – to become fragmented.

If your hard drive seems slow, you can use Disk Defragmenter in Windows 7 to rearrange the parts of large files to work more effectively. Disk Defragmenter can run at set times, and you can manually run it to defrag your hard drive as you need to.

Defrag your hard drive

1 Click the **Start** button. In the search box, type '**Disk Defragmenter**'. Click on **Disk Defragmenter** in the results list to open it.

2 Choose the disk to defragment from the list under **Current status**.

3 To see if the disk needs defragmenting, click **Analyze disk**. You may have to enter your administrator password at this point.

4 Once Disk Defragmenter has finished looking at your hard drive or disk, look at the percentage of fragmentation in the **Last Run** column. If the number is above 10%, then you need to defragment your disk.

5 Click **Defragment disk**. You may have to enter your administrator password at this point.

Depending on the size of the hard drive, the number of files and the types of files stored on the disk, it can take from a few minutes to several hours to defragment a disk with Disk Defragmenter. It is possible to continue to use your computer when Disk Defragmenter is running.

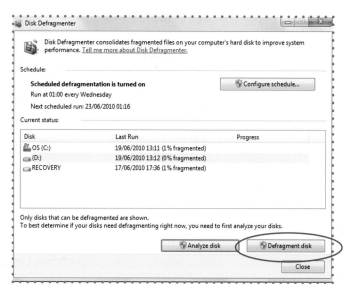

I can't defragment my hard drive

Sometimes Disk Defragmenter won't be able to defragment your disk. This is usually for one of several reasons:

▶ If the disk is already in exclusive use by another program or is formatted using a file system other than NTFS file system, FAT or FAT32, it can't be defragmented.

▶ Disks accessible on other computers over a network, such as another home PC, can't be defragmented. You would need to run Disk Defragment on the PC with the hard drive you want to defragment.

▶ If you can't see the hard drive you want to defragment listed under Current status, it might contain an error. Try to repair the disk (see page 148) and re-run Disk Defragment again.

MY HARD DRIVE ISN'T WORKING PROPERLY

Computer hard drives store all your long-term files and information
– but sometimes they can have problems that prevent the rest of your
computer from working, or prevent you from getting access to your files.

You can solve a few computer problems by checking a drive for errors
to help fix any performance problems (such as slow working). It's
also possible to check any external hard drive that you plug into your
computer to see if it isn't working properly.

Checking a hard drive for problems

1 Click the
Start button,
then click
Computer.

2 Right-click the
drive that you
want to check,
then choose
Properties
from the pop-up menu.

3 In the **Properties** panel, click the **Tools** tab, then under
Error-checking click **Check now...**. You may have to enter
your administrator password at this point.

The scan will now run and look for problems and errors with
the hard drive that you selected. If it finds and lists problems,
you can attempt to fix them there and then.

4 To automatically
fix the problems
with any folders
and files that the
scan reveals, tick
**Automatically
fix file system
errors**, then
click **Start**.

Performing a deeper check of the hard drive

If the quick scan of the hard drive in the previous steps doesn't resolve the issue, you can run a more thorough check of the hard drive:

1 Follow Steps 1 and 2 on page 192.

2 In the Properties panel, click the **Tools** tab, then under Error-checking tick **Scan for and attempt recovery of bad sectors**. You may have to enter your administrator password at this point. This scan can take a long time to complete, as it will attempt to find and repair physical problems with the hard drive itself.

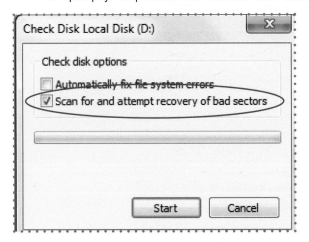

3 To check files, folders and also the hard drive for physical problems, tick both **Automatically fix file system errors** and **Scan for and attempt recovery of bad sectors**.

4 Click **Start**. Depending on the size of your drive and the number and type of files it contains, this might take several minutes. You should not use your computer for other tasks while the hard drive scan and repair is running.

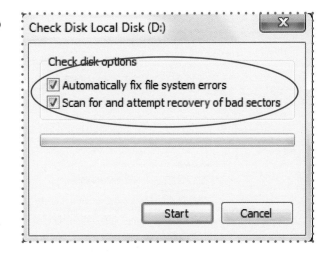

Keep your PC healthy

REINSTALLING WINDOWS 7

If you need to restore Windows 7 back to its original settings because it has a major, unfixable problem then you can either use System Restore to return it to a previous state (see page 180 for advice on this process) or reinstall Windows 7 and return your computer to its factory settings.

1 Click the **Start** button, then click **Control Panel**. Type '**recovery**' in the Control Panel search box. Click **Restore your computer or reinstall Windows** in the search results.

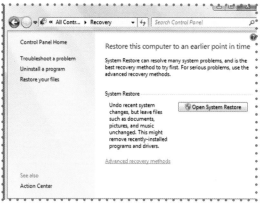

2 Click **Advanced recovery methods** in the window, then choose one of the following:

▶ **Use a system image you created earlier to recover your computer**
This will restore Windows and some of your personal settings and
files, such as photos in the Picture library, from a Backup and Restore
disc that you will need to have created earlier. See page 177 for help
on doing this.

▶ **Reinstall Windows (requires Windows installation disc)**
This will reinstall Windows 7 on your computer, but it will not delete
any user files. It will delete any programs you have installed since
Windows 7 was first installed, so you will need to reinstall these
afterwards. A new folder, called 'Windows.old' will be created that
stores all the user files so you can reapply settings once Windows 7
has been reinstalled.

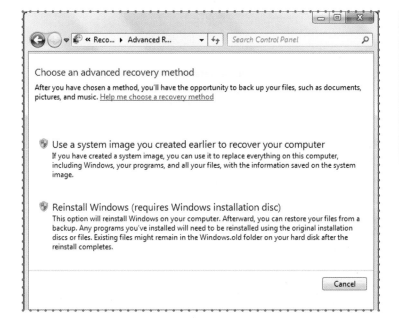

BE CAREFUL

Continuing will delete
data from your hard
drive, including personal
files and settings. Make
sure that you have a
full backup of valuable
information before you
continue. See page 176
for advice on backing up
your files.

Keep your PC healthy

RECOVERING DELETED FILES

If you've accidently deleted or changed a file, or it has gone missing from your computer, it is possible to recover it using System Restore from a backup location, or by performing a few basic checks.

Check the Recycle Bin

If you haven't emptied the Recycle Bin, which is usually located on the desktop, it is possible the file may be in the Bin and hasn't been deleted yet. To fix this:

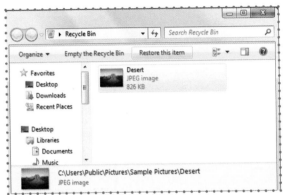

1 On the desktop, double-click the **Recycle Bin** and locate the file you need.

2 Select the file to be restored, then click **Restore this item**. It will reappear back in the location it was before it was placed in the Recycle Bin.

Restore deleted files using a backup location

If you are making regular backups of your files (see page 176 for help with backing up your files) you can restore a deleted file from your backup.

1 Click the **Start** button, then click **Control Panel**. Click **System and Security**, then click **Backup and Restore**.

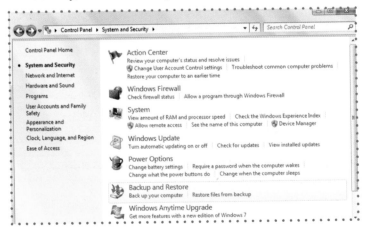

2 Click **Restore my files**, then follow the on-screen instructions. See page 180 for advice on restoring your PC.

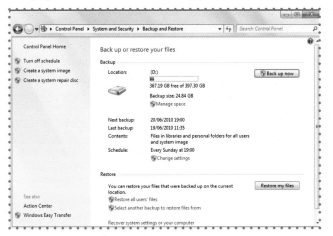

Recover a deleted file or folder

If you've accidentally deleted a folder or a file on your computer, Windows can use both backup and Restore points to restore a specific file. For advice on using Restore points, see page 180.

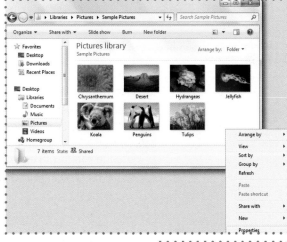

1 Click the **Start** button, then click **Computer**.

2 Locate the folder that used to contain the file or folder that has been deleted, and right-click it and choose **Properties**.

3 Under the **Previous Versions** tab, from the list of possible previous versions that appears, double-click a previous version of the folder that contained the file or folder you want to restore. Click **Restore...**.

4 Drag the folder or file to another location, such as another folder. The file or folder will then be saved to that new destination, ready to be used.

MY PC IS RUNNING SLOWLY

If your computer is running slowly and performing tasks with less speed than previously, Windows 7 offers several tools and settings that can help add more speed to your computer.

Using Performance Information and Tasks to boost speed

The easiest route to speeding up your PC is to change some of its performance settings to lessen the load on the computer's processor and increase its speed:

1 Click the **Start** button, then click **Control Panel**.

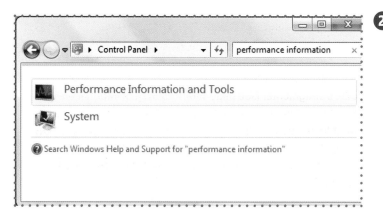

2 In the search box in Control Panel, type '**Performance Information**' and then, in the results list that appears, click **Performance Information and Tools**.

3 Choose a setting from the table shown below and opposite and use the controls to adjust it for increased performance according to the on-screen instructions.

Setting	Description
Adjust visual effects	Changes how windows and menus appear – lower settings will speed up your PC.
Adjust indexing options	This sets how Windows indexes the files on your PC so you can find them using search.
Adjust power settings	Useful for laptops so you can increase speed at the expense of battery life.
Open disk cleanup	This deletes unnecessary or temporary files on your hard disk so you can increase the amount of storage space you have.
Advanced tools	Gives access to more advanced tools, such as Event Viewer, Disk Defragmenter (see page 190), and System Information. You can see information about performance-related issues and what to do about them. For example, if a driver is causing a slow computer, click the notification to learn which driver is causing the problem and view help on how to update the driver (see page 186).

Other steps to take

There are a few other steps you can take to increase the speed of your computer:

▶ **Add extra RAM**

Find out whether you can upgrade your PC's RAM. The website www.crucial.com is a handy way of identifying the type and amount of memory you can add to your PC. Fitting extra RAM isn't too tricky, but you may want to seek expert help if you're worried.

▶ **Update your operating system**

Using an old version of the Windows operating system can slow down your computer substantially. If you're still using Windows XP or Windows Vista, for example, it may be time to upgrade.

TEN PC HOUSEKEEPING TIPS

Keeping a PC running smoothly can be dramatically helped by ensuring that you follow a routine in computer housekeeping. Below are ten must-do activities that will help keep your PC running better for longer. Where more information on performing these tasks is located elsewhere in this book, refer to the page number listed.

1 **Get rid of unwanted programs**

Many computers come with lots of extra programs when you buy them, including trial versions of software packages, trial subscriptions to anti-virus packages, and limited editions of software that manufacturers hope will entice you to upgrade to the full version. These can take up lots of memory and storage space, so look at uninstalling programs that you don't think you'll use. See How to remove programs on page 50.

2 **Limit the number of programs that run at startup**

Lots of programs will start running invisibly in the background when you turn on your computer – leading to potential crashes and sometimes slower performance. You can turn off those you don't need quite easily.
See Disabling startup conflicts on page 24.

3 **Routinely restart your computer**

Restarting your PC weekly clears out its memory and means that any memory problems get wiped clear. It also closes all the programs that are running on the PC, including hidden programs running in the background – so it's a good starting point if your computer seems to be behaving strangely.

To restart your computer, click the **Start** button and click the arrow in the bottom-right of the **Start Menu**. From the menu, choose **Restart**.

4 Keep programs in check

It may seem convenient to keep on top of your activities by having lots of programs and windows open at the same time, but its worth closing windows and programs you aren't really using. Lots of web browser windows and email messages being shown on screen will bog down your computer. Close down unneeded programs for a speed boost.

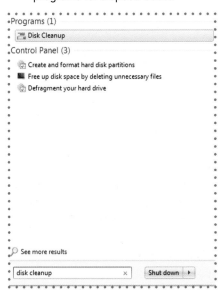

5 Keep your hard drive free of clutter

It's relatively easy to fill up your hard drive with lots of unneeded files, such as temporary files stored by a web browser. But lots of these files can slow down your hard drive, so use Disk Cleanup to remove unneeded files. To delete files using Disk Cleanup:

a. Click the **Start** button and in the search box type '**Disk Cleanup**', and click **Disk Cleanup** from the results list that appears.

b. In the window that appears, click the hard drive picture for the hard drive you want to clean, then click **OK**.

c. Select the types of files you'd like to delete using the tick boxes, then click **OK** and then, in the box that appears, click **Delete files**.

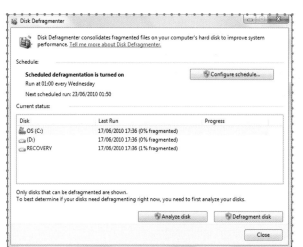

6 **Regularly defragment your hard drive**

When your computer stores a large file on the hard drive, it can sometimes break it up into smaller parts and place each part in different locations on the hard drive. This can make the hard drive run slower, but Windows 7 includes a Disk Defragmenter tool that can be set to run at scheduled times as part of your regular cycle of PC housekeeping. See Defrag your hard drive on page 190.

7 **Check for viruses and spyware**

As part of PC housekeeping, remember to run your anti-virus software regularly to check for viruses and spyware that may have installed on your computer without you knowing. Viruses can make your PC run more slowly and possibly compromise your valuable data, or display messages on the screen. Spyware can track your movements on the web, and some types can record the key strokes you make on your keyboard in a bid to uncover passwords and other valuable data.

See How to check a PC for a virus on page 124.

8 **Delete old emails**

Trawling through old emails is a bit of a drag but it'll free up valuable space on your hard disk. To delete an email in Outlook, right-click on the message in the inbox and select **Delete**. If you want to delete a chunk of messages, click on the first message, hold down the Shift button and click on the last message. The messages will be highlighted. Right-click on the messages and click **Delete** as before.

Deleted emails go into the Deleted Items folder. To completely delete them, click **Tools**, then click **Empty "Deleted Items" Folder**.

⑨ Clean up your desktop

It's quicker and easier to find things on a tidy desk and your computer's no different. When you install a new program, it'll invariably add an icon – a shortcut to open the program – to your PC's desktop. It's not long, though, before your Windows desktop is crammed with icons for programs that you no longer use. So it's time for a cleanup.

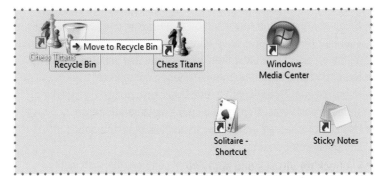

Identify the shortcuts you don't need, click on an unwanted icon on the desktop, and drag and drop it into the Recycle Bin. A shortcut has a small arrow in the lower-left corner. Deleting a shortcut will not delete the original program.

⑩ Remember to empty your Recycle Bin

Your Recycle Bin is an area of your hard disk where you store 'deleted' files. Files can be recovered from here and are still occupying precious hard disk space; to free up this space empty the Recycle Bin. Before emptying your bin, make certain you really don't need what you're deleting.

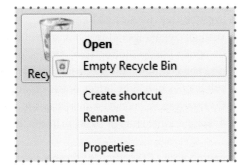

To empty the bin, double-click the icon on your desktop. On the **File** menu click **Empty Recycle Bin**.

⊳ Keep your PC healthy

CLEANING YOUR COMPUTER AND DEVICES

As well as computer bugs and software glitches, some problems can be more physical in nature. Dirt, dust and general day-to-day use can see a build up of unwanted grime on your computer, screen and devices. Here's a guide to keeping everything sparkling.

Dos and don'ts

▶ Turn off the computer and screen and let it cool before cleaning.
▶ Never spray or squirt any liquid on or near your computer. To apply a liquid (preferably water or an approved computer cleaning fluid), put a little on a soft cloth first then wipe the surface with the cloth.
▶ Never dampen any component inside the computer.
▶ Use a vacuum cleaner with a rubber or brush nozzle on exterior surfaces and vents. Don't use it inside the computer case.
▶ Use compressed air in short bursts to blow dust and debris off computer components.
▶ Clean gently: don't bump any internal components such as the motherboard or video board.
▶ Don't use a cloth to wipe down internal computer components.
▶ Don't smoke near a computer. Smoke particles can lead to corrosion and component failure.

Preparation

Before you start cleaning, shut down the computer and unplug it. You'll need the following tools to clean your computer:
▶ Foam-tip applicators (such as eye shadow applicators) or cotton buds (be careful of leaving behind wispy bits of cotton)
▶ Lint-free cloth (or alcohol-free wipes)
▶ Vacuum cleaner (preferably with soft rubber or brush attachments)
▶ Computer brush (a retractable soft bristle anti-static brush for cleaning computer parts, or a new small household paintbrush with soft bristles or a large artists brush will do)
▶ Compressed air (available in pressurized cans from computer stores)
▶ Anti-static wrist strap (if cleaning inside the PC case).

Cleaning your LCD computer screen

LCD screens are particularly easy to damage, so go easy with the pressure when wiping.

 Start by gently wiping the screen with a soft, lint-free cloth.

2 If needed, lightly dampen (not wet) the cloth with a small amount of water. You can also use anti-static screen wipes, available from computer stores.

Cleaning your keyboard

Crumbs! You'd be surprised how many of these find their way inside your keyboard, especially if you eat lunch at your desk.

1 Unplug your keyboard, turn it upside down and shake out any loose dust and food crumbs inside.

2 To remove the remaining debris, spray between the keys with a compressed air can or vacuum it using a rubber or brush-type nozzle.

3 You can also use a computer brush (or new small paint brush) to sweep between the keys.

4 Next, wipe down the surface with a lightly dampened (not wet) cloth or use foam-tip applicators lightly dampened with water.

Alcohol wipes will rid your keyboard of bacteria. Alcohol-free wipes are gentler on your keyboard and won't rub letters off but only alcohol wipes will rid your keyboard of germs.

Cleaning your computer mouse

Use a puff of compressed air to blow lint and dust off the optical sensor or gently wipe it with a slightly damp foam-tipped applicator or cotton bud. Finally, clean any non-stick 'feet', as dirt can build up here.

Cleaning computer casing

You can wipe over the outside case of a desktop or laptop with a damp cloth and use a vacuum cleaner to clear any vents of dust. Use a small brush head on the vacuum cleaner and run it slowly over the vents.

Keeping the area around your computer clean is vital to a healthy cooling system where fans suck air in through vents at the front of the case and expel it at the back, cooling the internal components along the way. If your computer is over a year old or in a dusty environment you may want to unplug it and remove the casing (if this doesn't void your warranty).

Keep your PC healthy

BE CAREFUL

When cleaning an LCD screen, don't use domestic cleaning products or wipes containing alcohol as these can damage the anti-glare coating on LCD screens. Also, don't use paper towels as these can be abrasive.

BE CAREFUL

It's an internet myth that you can clean your keyboard by popping it in the dishwasher. It will clean your keyboard, but it probably won't work again.

BE CAREFUL

Never use a vacuum cleaner inside a PC as it can damage components, and don't attempt to open the casing of a laptop as it can void your warranty. Finally, don't touch internal components of your computer.

Make sure you use an antistatic wrist strap (available from computer and electronics stores) and carefully clean the internal components using short bursts of compressed air.

Cleaning your CD or DVD drive

Dust, fibres and hair inside your drive can cause problems recording to and playing discs. Wipe the exterior opening and tray of your optical drive with a dry cloth, and use a CD/DVD cleaning disc to clean inside the disc drive.

Cleaning your earphones

Headphones used by multiple people can spread germs or even head lice. Wipe them with a damp cloth, or preferably don't share them with others at all.

ESSENTIAL SOFTWARE

By reading and following all the steps in this chapter, you will get to grips with:

- Downloading free programs from Microsoft that will enhance your computer

- Downloading and using free Microsoft security software to protect from viruses

- Downloading and using free family protection programs

MICROSOFT SECURITY ESSENTIALS

If you need to protect your computer with basic security tools and protection, Microsoft includes a collection of security essentials designed to help stop malware from harming your computer.

What's included in Microsoft Security Essentials

Microsoft Security Essentials is a free download from Microsoft that helps Windows 7 guard against problem and dangerous software such as spyware and viruses. Once downloaded, it installs itself and runs quietly in the background, alerting you to potential problems and malware, and preventing spyware and viruses.

While it isn't a replacement for a comprehensive security software suite that you'd buy in the shops, such as Symantec Norton Internet Security, it does include real-time protection. This means that Microsoft Security Essentials keeps itself up to date with the latest security threats and will automatically update itself as needed.

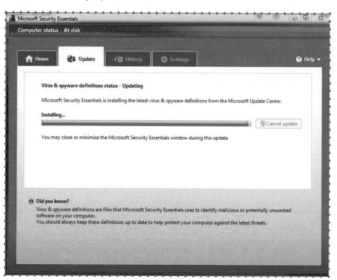

TRY THIS

If you'd like to find out more about the threats being tackled by Microsoft Security Essentials then visit www.microsoft.com/security/portal/

What requirements does my computer need to have?

You need to be running Windows 7 on a computer that has a 1 GHz or faster processor, 1 GB of RAM or more, 140 MB of free hard drive space, and an internet connection to download the software and ensure it keeps up to date.

Download from www.microsoft.com/security_essentials/

WINDOWS LIVE FAMILY SAFETY

If you're concerned about ensuring children using your computer are safe when using the internet, and would like to get up-to-date reports on their online activities, then the free-to-download Windows Live Family Safety is a useful addition to Windows 7.

What's included in Windows Live Family Safety

Central to Windows Live Family Safety is a content filter that works to stop children accessing inappropriate websites. The content filter can be customized, allowing you to set different levels of access to different types of websites.

Also included are activity reports so you can keep tabs on what your children are up to on the internet, and everything can be controlled through a web browser, so you can change settings from any location that has a computer connected to the internet. You can also manage who children can contact online using instant messaging software.

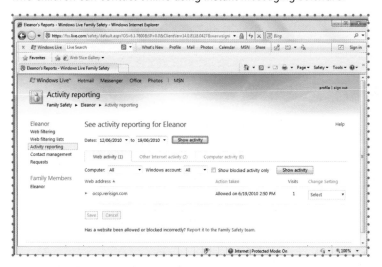

What requirements does my computer need to have?

You need to be running Windows 7 on a computer that has a 1 GHz or faster processor, 512 MB of RAM or more, a screen resolution of at least 1024 × 768, Internet Explorer 6 or higher, and an internet connection to download the software.

Download from www.windowslive.co.uk/familysafety.aspx

TRY THIS

The best way to protect children online is to have positive, open communication with them so they understand their boundaries, and can flag any concerns with you as soon as possible.

essential software

Jargon buster

Webmail
Email accounts accessed through your web browser. Email is not stored locally on your computer.

TRY THIS

If you want to add a background image to an email in **Windows Live Mail**, click **Format**, then click **Background**, then click **Image...**.
Use the **Browse...** button to locate the desired image. Click **OK** when done.

WINDOWS LIVE MAIL

If you don't want to use a webmail account that stores your email online, then it's worth using Microsoft Windows Live Mail. This free-to-download software allows multiple email accounts from Hotmail, Gmail and Yahoo! accounts to be managed in one place.

What's included in Windows Live Mail

Windows Live Mail provides a way to read and control a Hotmail email account and contacts (which is free to set up) while you are offline, so you don't need an internet connection to be able to read older email. It can also manage email from other email services, such as Gmail and Yahoo!, and store email locally on your hard drive.

Other features include the ability to optimize photos when attaching them to email and add effects such as captions and borders, and send high-quality photos without the recipient having their email account filled with lots of big attachments. It can also get content, such as news feeds, delivered to your inbox from websites.

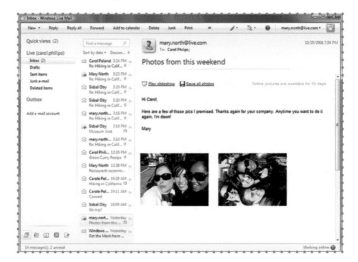

What requirements does my computer need to have?

You need to be running Windows 7 on a computer that has a 1 GHz or faster processor, 512 MB of RAM or more, a screen resolution of at least 1024 × 768, Internet Explorer 6 or higher, and an internet connection to download the software.

Download from http://download.live.com/wlmail

WINDOWS LIVE MOVIE MAKER

Windows Movie Maker was a standard feature of previous versions of Windows, but it was not included in Windows 7. Microsoft instead wants users to download its newer Windows Live Movie Maker. The good news is that the software is free and includes lots of tools for editing and sharing videos.

What's included in Windows Live Movie Maker

Designed as a basic video-editing program, Windows Live Movie Maker includes the ability to mix together video from a camcorder, as well as digital photos and music from the Music library in Windows 7 to make a home movie. It includes some basic editing features, such as adding titles, credits, effects and transitions, including panning and zooming.

Other features include the ability to create animated slideshows from your photo collection, and publish your finished film or slideshow directly onto the internet to sites such as YouTube. If you are using Windows 7 Home Premium, you can also create DVDs of your films.

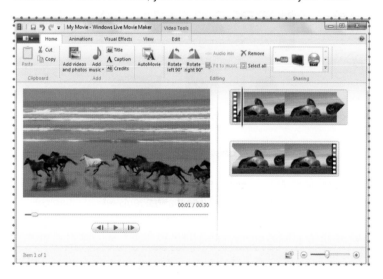

What requirements does my computer need to have?

You need to be running Windows 7 on a computer that has a 1 GHz or faster processor, 512 MB of RAM or more, a screen resolution of at least 1024 × 768, Internet Explorer 6 or higher, and an internet connection to download the software.

Download from http://download.live.com/MovieMaker

▶ Essential software

TRY THIS

If you right-click an empty area of a gallery in Windows Live Photo Gallery and choose Group by, you can group your photos by date, file size, rating, person, camera used, tag and more.

WINDOWS LIVE PHOTO GALLERY

Many Windows 7 users upgrading from a previous version of Windows were dismayed to find out that Windows Photo Gallery was no longer included. The good news is that it is available for free from Microsoft as a download, and provides a series of tools to import, manage, edit and share your photos.

What's included in Windows Live Photo Gallery

Providing a one-stop shop for managing your photos, Windows Live Photo Gallery includes tools to organize, edit and share photos. For help and advice using Windows Live Photo Gallery, see page 154.

Tools include an Auto Adjust option that tries to automatically improve the quality of your photos, as well as manual tools for changing colour, detail and exposure. You can rate and tag photos for easy finding, as well as share photos online, email them to friends and family or order prints from the photos.

What requirements does my computer need to have?

You need to be running Windows 7 on a computer that has a 1 GHz or faster processor, 1 GB of RAM or more, 140 MB of free hard drive space, and an internet connection to download the software and ensure it keeps up to date.

Download from http://download.live.com/photogallery

RESOURCES

▶ Jargon buster

3G The third generation of mobile networks, which allows large amounts of data to be sent wirelessly. Mobile broadband operates over the 3G network.

ADSL (Asymmetric Digital Subscriber Line) A way of sending data over a copper wire telephone line.

Adware Software that tracks your web use to determine your interests and deliver relevant adverts.

Anti-spyware Software that prevents and/or removes spyware.

Anti-virus Software that scans for viruses and removes them from your computer.

Application see **Program**.

Attachment A computer file that is sent along with an email message. It can be any type of software file, and can be opened by the receiver if the appropriate software to view the file attachment is installed or available.

Backup A copy of your files or programs for safekeeping.

Bitmap screen font file Shows a digital version of a letter made up of tiny dots called pixels. While this is suitable for the screen, when printed out a bitmap file tends to look jagged.

Blog A regularly updated online diary or journal.

Bluetooth A type of short range, wireless connection for transferring data between devices.

Bookmarks A collection of favourite websites visited and saved by the user.

Broadband A method of connecting to the internet via cable or ADSL. Much faster than a dial-up connection.

Browser The software that enables you to view webpages. Often contains phishing filters.

Browser history A folder that is stored by the browser, which contains details of recently visited websites.

Buffer A portion of computer memory used by a program as a temporary storage area for information being used immediately and then replaced by more information.

Cache The way web browsers store recently-accessed pages, images, and other data so they can be displayed rapidly the next time they're requested.

Card reader A device for reading data stored on memory cards, such as used by digital cameras.

Case sensitive Most search tools are not case sensitive or only respond to initial capitals, as in proper names. But as capital letters (upper case) retrieve only upper case, it's best to type lower case (no capitals) because lower case will always retrieve upper case letters too.

CD-R/RW Drive A Compact Disk Recordable or ReWritable can record data, images or music files onto blank discs.

Control panel A series of dedicated programs that adjust the computer's settings, such as passwords, internet access and accessibility.

Cookie A piece of information sent to a user's web browser by a website. The web browser then returns that information to the website. This is how some websites 'remember' your previous visits.

Cursor The symbol on the screen that shows you where the next character you type will appear.

Desktop The main screen you see when you start your computer. From here you can organize and access programs and files.

Dial-up An internet connection via a normal phone line, which is slow compared with broadband.

Dongle A small device that connects to a computer's USB port and enables you to connect to the internet.

Download To transfer data from a remote computer to your own computer over the internet.

Drive letter Each drive on your computer, such as the hard drive and CD drive, is assigned a different letter to help you recognize which drive is which. Typically, your internal hard drive is assigned the letter C, while DVD or CD drives will be assigned the letter E or F.

Driver Software that allows your computer to communicate with other devices, such as a printer.

DRM (Digital Rights Management) Software that limits the number of copies you can make of a particular piece of music.

DVD-R/RW drive Optical drive that can read and write to DVD discs.

Email client A computer program that manages emails. Emails are stored on your computer, and you only need to be connected to the internet to send and receive emails.

Ethernet A means of connecting computers together using cables – a common method for networking computers.

External hard drive A storage device that plugs into your PC. Useful for saving copies of important files or creating additional storage.

FAQs Frequently Asked Questions.

File extension The letters that appear after a file name. They show what type of document it is and what type of program will open it – for example, a Microsoft Word document will end in .doc.

Firewall Software (or hardware) that blocks unwanted communication from, and often to, the internet.

Flash content A type of interactive content, such as an animated cartoon. Interactive, animated parts of a web page, such as a game, animation or interactive presentation is usually created in a format called 'Flash'.

Flash drive see **Memory stick**.

Forum An online message board for chatting or posting questions and opinions.

FTP (File Transfer Protocol) Ability to transfer rapidly entire files from one computer to another, for viewing or other purposes.

GB (Gigabyte) A measurement of data storage. Eight bits make up a byte; 1,024 bytes make a kilobyte; 1,024 kilobytes make a megabyte; and 1,024 megabytes make a gigabyte.

Hard disk The main long-term storage space used by your computer to store data. Also known as a hard drive.

Hard drive see **Hard disk**.

Hardware Physical equipment, such as a computer, screen or printer.

▶ Jargon buster

Homegroup This is the name Windows 7 gives to a home wireless network; it assumes that it is a secure network and that all devices on it are trusted.

Icon A small picture that represents an object or program.

ISP (Internet Service Provider) The company that enables and services your connection to the internet.

Link Short for hyperlink, a link can be either text or an image that lets you jump straight to another webpage when you click on it.

Log in/out To log in or sign in is to provide a username and password to identify yourself to a website. To log out or sign out is to notify the site that you're no longer using it, which will deny you (and other people who might subsequently use your web browser) access to the functions until you log in again.

Malware Malicious software. A generic term for any program that is harmful to your computer, for example, a virus.

MB (Megabyte) A measurement of data storage. Eight bits make up a byte; 1,024 bytes make a kilobyte; 1,024 kilobytes make a megabyte.

Mbps (Megabits per second) A measure of the speed of data transfer, often used when talking about the speed of broadband.

Memory card A removable storage device, which holds images taken with a camera. They come in a variety of sizes and there are several types including Compact Flash, Multimedia and SD cards as well as Sony's Memory Stick format.

Memory stick A small, portable device used to store and transfer data. It plugs into a USB port and is sometimes called a USB key, flash drive or pen drive.

MHz (Megahertz) The speed of your computer's processor is measured in megahertz. One MHz represents one million cycles per second.

Microfilter A device that attaches to your telephone socket and enables you to make voice calls and use broadband at the same time via ADSL.

Modem A device that allows a computer to send information over a telephone line.

MP3 The standard file format for digital music. The attraction of the format is that it is not tied to any one manufacturer in the way that AAC (Apple) and WMA (Microsoft) are.

MP3 player A portable music player that plays digital music.

Network A system of communication between two or more computers.

News tickers Usually ribbons or lines of scrolling text that appear across the bottom or top of the browser window. Typically, they show scrolling text from news organizations, such as CNN or the BBC.

Operating system The software that manages your computer and the environment that programs operate in.

PDA (Personal Digital Assistant) Typically, a small, handheld digital device for storing contacts, calendar and emails.

PDF A type of file that captures all the graphics, fonts and formatting of a document, regardless of the application in which it was created.

Phishing A type of email scam where you're tricked into giving away personal details by being directed to a spoof website that resembles the site of an official organization (a bank, for example).

Pinned shortcut Windows 7 uses the terminology 'pinned' to mean a program icon that is added to and always appears in the taskbar. It refers to the program as being, effectively, 'pinned' to the task bar, like being pinned to a notice board, for easy and quick access.

POP3 (Post Office Protocol) A way of allowing an email server (a computer dedicated to delivering email) to 'post' emails to your computer.

Pop-up A small window that appears over an item (word or picture) on your computer screen to give additional information.

Port A computer socket into which you plug equipment.

Processor The main computer chip that controls and carries out the functions of a computer. The better the processor, the more a computer can do in a given amount of time.

Program Computer software that performs a specific task, such as a word processor or photo editor. Programs run in Windows, and are launched from the Start menu.

RAM (Random Access Memory) The short-term memory of the computer which holds all running programs.

Router A device that routes data between computers and other devices. Routers can connect computers to each other or connect a computer to the internet.

Secure website A site that you can trust is what it says it is. Any personal details that you enter are encrypted – scrambled so cybercrooks can't read them – between your computer and the website in question.

Security suite A bundle of security programs to protect your PC.

SMTP (Simple Mail Transfer Protocol) A standard internet protocol allowing an email program on your computer to deliver outgoing emails to an online email server (such as a webmail service).

Social networking A way for people to socialize online, typically via a website, such as Facebook or Bebo.

Software A general term for programs used to operate computers and related devices.

Spam Unsolicited junk email.

Spam filter A system that helps to keep spam out of your email inbox.

Spyware Software that secretly installs on your computer and is able to track your internet behaviour and send details to a third party.

Start button A round icon with the Windows logo in it, located in the lower left-hand corner of your screen.

System tray An area on your Windows desktop that displays program icons and alerts you when action is required.

▶ Jargon buster

Taskbar The bar running across the bottom of your screen, from where you can open programs and access the main Windows functions.

Toolbar A vertical or horizontal onscreen bar that's made up of small icons that, when clicked, will perform a task.

Trojan A computer virus that disguises itself as an innocent program to entice people to install it. Trojans can allow third parties complete access to your computer remotely.

Upload The process of sending files from your computer to the internet.

URL (Uniform Resource Locator) A website's 'address'.

USB (Universal Serial Bus) A connection technology that allows you to transfer data easily between a computer and a device, such as a camera or printer. USB cables are used to connect devices and are plugged into a USB port on your computer.

USB key see **Memory stick**.

Username Also called a login name, screen name or login, it is a unique name used to identify a person online.

Video adaptor A PC component that sends data from the computer to the screen and displays it as the image you see.

Virus A malevolent program that spreads from computer to computer within another program or file.

Wallpaper A digital photo or image that is used as a backdrop to the Windows 7 desktop.

Web browser see **Browser**

Webmail Email accounts that are accessed through your web browser. Email is not stored locally on your computer.

Webpage Each website on the internet usually has more than one page, these are referred to as webpages. Each webpage has a unique address that you type in to go directly to that page.

Wi-Fi A wireless, high-speed networking system that can transfer data at high speeds across lots of different devices.

Wizard A software helper that will guide you through a series of on-screen steps to help you set up or change the settings of a part of Windows, such as your firewall.

World Wide Web Frequently shortened to just the web or WWW, the World Wide Web refers to the billions of websites that are hosted on servers all over the world and are accessible via web browsers. The term 'web' indicates the billions of webpages that link to one another.

▶ Index

⏵ Index

▶ Index